YIN-YANG IN TAI-CHI CHUAN AND DAILY LIFE

Other Books by Simmone Kuo

Long Life, Good Health through T'ai Chi Ch'uan
Shao-Lin Chuan: The Rhythm and Power of Tan-Tui

By Kuo Lien-Ying

Tai-Chi Chuan in Theory and Practice (edited by Simmone Kuo)

Yin-Yang in Tai-Chi Chuan and Daily Life

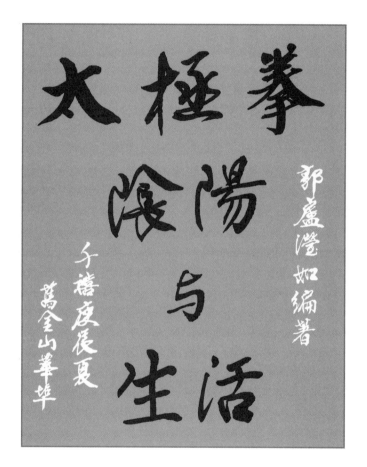

Simmone Kuo

NORTH ATLANTIC BOOKS
BERKELEY, CALIFORNIA

Published by
North Atlantic Books
P.O. Box 12327
Berkeley, California 94712
www.northatlanticbooks.com

Cover and text design by Susan Quasha
Image on front cover from a painting by Yao You-Wei

Printed in The United States of America
Distributed to the book trade by Publishers Group West

Yin-Yang in Tai-Chi Chuan and Daily Life is sponsored by the Society for the Study of
Native Arts and Sciences, a nonprofit educational corporation whose goals are to develop
an educational and crosscultural perspective linking various scientific, social, and artistic
fields; to nurture a holistic view of arts, sciences, humanities, and healing; and to publish and
distribute literature on the relationship of mind, body, and nature.

Library of Congress Cataloging-in-Publication Data

Kuo, Simmone.
  Yin-yang in tai-chi chuan and daily life / by Simmone Kuo.
    p. cm.
  Includes bibliographical references.
  ISBN 1-55643-516-9 (pbk.)
  1. Yin-yang. 2. Tai chi. I. Title.

  B127.Y56.K855 2004
  613.7'148—dc22
2004015981

1 2 3 4 5 6 7 DATA 08 07 06 05 04

Contents

This book is dedicated to my parents, especially to my mother,
who has shown me a model of perseverance, integrity, and arduous work.
I would also like to thank my father, who refused to sell me during times of economic trouble.

Simmone Kuo and her mother, Hung-Lan (Buddhist name meaning "Orchid of Perseverance"), A-Hsiang W. Lu (given name)

Tai-Chi Chuan is passed on to the new generation.

Author's Introduction to
Yin-Yang in Tai-Chi Chuan and Daily Life

SIMMONE KUO

For more than thirty years now, I have been practicing and teaching Tai-Chi Chuan. A vital part of my study has been ongoing research into the Yin-Yang philosophy, which is at the foundation of all traditional Chinese culture. Along with medical practice, agriculture, and statesmanship, the development of Chinese martial arts was shaped by the application of Yin-Yang philosophy. Indeed, the name "Tai-Chi Chuan" means the martial art (*chuan* = fist) based on the balancing of Yin and Yang energies *(Tai-Chi)*.

My research has included extensive travel in China, where I've come in contact with many valuable sources. Some of what I've discovered on these trips is pictured in this book. Above all, though, I learned directly from Sifu Kuo Lien-Ying, my teacher and late husband. During our twenty years of marriage, I had the opportunity to consult with him regarding all my questions. More important, I was privileged to share in the life of a great master, and to observe his manner of applying Yin-Yang philosophy to all aspects of daily life.

Much of the material included in this book was initially presented in the form of weekly lectures to my advanced class in Tai-Chi Chuan at San Francisco State University. Just as the lectures there are complementary to the twice-weekly practice sessions, so this volume is a companion to *Long Life, Good Health through Tai-Chi Chuan*. That volume depicts, in detail, the movements of the Tai-Chi Chuan form. The current volume focuses on how the philosophical roots of the art are applied in daily life—to self-care, for instance, and to daily practice—in order to live in harmony with the world of nature and of human society.

The knowledge conveyed here provides a background method for integrating body and mind—Yin and Yang—so that students can develop the balance and wisdom needed to live healthy and fulfilling lives. As a teacher, one always hopes that the next generation will receive the teaching and create something better, without sacrificing what is essential. I am proud to have several students who have remained true to this teaching, and who care for the integrity of the form and the tradition of knowledge it embodies.

I feel as if I helped to plant a tree together with Sifu, many years ago. Now I am watching a whole forest grow. So many of our dreams have come true! It is my pleasure to share some of the experience I've gained in the realization of these dreams. This book is an offering, a gift to the many dedicated students of Tai-Chi Chuan. May their practice deepen and flourish, and the benefit increase, radiating in all directions.

Introduction to Simmone Kuo

DANIEL RYBOLD

Master Simmone Kuo, or Simu—meaning "female teacher"—as she is more properly and fondly addressed by those of us who study with her, has been teaching Tai-Chi Chuan in the heart of San Francisco's Chinatown for the past thirty-five years. For the last thirteen of these I have had the great good fortune of deepening my own practice of the form with her. Perhaps it would be more correct to say that since I moved to San Francisco in 1987 to complete my family practice residency at San Francisco General Hospital, and more recently to take up the practices of acupuncture and energetic bodywork, Simu has helped me shape and reclaim the various landscapes of life informed by my form.

Simu has not only been an extraordinary practitioner and teacher of Tai-Chi Chuan during these many years, she has also gracefully—and with tremendous grit and determination—brought the form to literally thousands of students at San Francisco State University (where she began the first class of its kind in the state of California in 1980), authored several books on related practices (including the most recently published *Tai-Chi Chuan in Theory and Practice,* honoring her late husband Grand Master Kuo Lien-Ying—known as Sifu, or "male teacher"), hosted a TV show in the East Bay, raised her talented son Chung Mei (who himself inspired the first students at the square with his natural talent and gift of enthusiasm), and led various groups on cultural tours—*all* while keeping her Portsmouth Square Studio on Walter U. Lum Place open to those of us who continued our studies of this life-transforming discipline with her.

Perhaps the fact that Simu and Sifu donated the building next door to their studio to the Chinese Affirmative Action Cultural Center, a gift that benefits many citizens of San Francisco's Chinese community, will paint for you a clearer picture of Simmone's generous and caring nature. I will finish simply by saying that it is with heartfelt gratitude and an ever-growing conviction in the application of these profound and beautiful movements to the entirety of my life that I humbly dedicate any merits of my practice to the long and healthy life of my Simu, Master Simmone Kuo. I trust that by reading this book you too will receive the benefits and joy contained in her knowledge.

Foreword

John Bratten, Ph.D., Gerontology

My esteemed teacher, Simmone Kuo, has imparted much knowledge to me over the years. It was under her guidance that I developed self-confidence and an awareness of my own teaching ability by participating as her assistant in her classes at San Francisco State University. Prior to my assistantship, I had studied Tai-Chi Chuan for one calendar year with Simmone Kuo—or Simu ("Simu" is a title of respect meaning "female teacher")—first as a student in one of her classes at SFSU during the 1991–92 academic year, and continuing studies with her privately during the summer of 1992. Near the end of the '92 spring semester, Simu invited me to be her teaching assistant for the fall semester, and I accepted with pleasure and pride.

The writer/philosopher Kahlil Gibran said the following about teaching:

> No man can reveal to you aught but that which already lies half
> asleep in the dawning of your knowledge.
> The teacher who walks in the shadow of the temple, among his
> followers, gives not of his wisdom but rather of his faith and his
> lovingness.
> If he is indeed wise he does not bid you enter the house of his
> wisdom, but rather leads you to the threshold of your own mind.

My relationship with Simu has been the catalyst for some of my most valuable learning. She has been my friend always, and perhaps the primary consequence of our friendship as it has affected my studies has been its positive effect on my motivation to practice Tai-Chi Chuan. My ability to learn this "internal" martial art was jeopardized from the beginning by my lifelong tendency not to follow through with studies and disciplines regardless of my initial degree of interest or attraction. Simu very gently, and almost imperceptibly, led me to the threshold of my own self-motivation. Several times during the first year of studies of Tai-Chi Chuan, I was near the familiar point where I would give up (partly out of pure laziness, and partly out of shyness of participating in group activities) and simply cease attending classes. At first it was my attraction to Simu—to her fun, warm sense of humor and her gentle yet strong teaching style—that kept me returning. Later, it was our friendship, a friendship that she fostered and carefully nurtured, a type of friendship she has with several of her students.

From the beginning Simu evoked a special faith in me that this study of Tai-Chi Chuan would yield great benefits and that I should continue with it. Though her words of encouragement are powerful—for example, her reminder that "Tai-Chi Chuan is like American Social Security: you practice, practice every day and it's like money in the bank for when you're old so you will have a good health and long life"—still, it is her actions that fostered the strongest faith in me. Those actions were not even intentional. The day I first met her, for example, I was searching for the Tai-Chi class at Cox Field, where it was scheduled to be, and I showed up at the top of the bleachers on the south side of the field. I was expecting a male teacher. There was only one person anywhere around, and that person had her back to me, looking out over Cox Field, obviously a woman, with her hair in a bun. I approached her to inquire about the class. She seemed to sense my approach and turned fully to face me, and I knew instantly that here was the teacher, and that I was going to like her. In the simple action of turning around, this woman showed extraordinary strength, confidence, and grace of movement. She turned around with a smile already on her face and her eyes shining and eager to meet whoever it was that approached. It was as if she were expecting me, as if I were an old and very dear friend. My faith in her skill as a teacher and the power of her art has never faltered since.

In the very beginning I think I expected magical benefits. Soon the practice began to seem like a lot of work, and the benefits weren't proving to be magical at all, though I did realize many practical ones, such as improved balance and a new sense of grace in my movements. I pushed myself through prescribed daily practices; between my own efforts and the faith that Simu so beautifully evoked, I continued through to the point that, six months after beginning, I had learned the entire 64-movement form, and was finally a beginning student of Tai-Chi Chuan. And there stood Simu, beaming at my class; I remember feeling that now the real work was to begin, and here was our teacher ready to keep pumping up the faith, ready to work just as hard as we were ready. She was with us.

And I've felt like that about Simu ever since: She is willing to work just as hard with me as I am willing to work with me. She will meet the amount of energy I put into my practice, no matter how much energy that is. She can do this almost effortlessly, and this is part of what I consider her "magic." Actually, it is part of her wisdom, and it is part of the wisdom of her martial art. It is a part of that in her which is the Master. I think she is willing to work like this for me because she loves me, as she loves all of her dedicated students. This love is also a part of her that is the Master, perhaps the largest part.

This love, in my case, manifests in one form as deep friendship, in another form as relationship between a devoted student and his devoted teacher, and in another form as relationship between a dedicated teacher and her dedicated assistant. It has been my most thorough pleasure—indeed, it has been my bliss—to be Simmone Kuo's teaching assistant during this semester.

As my assistantship began, I strived to be as "mechanically" correct as possible. That is, as Tai-Chi Chuan is comprised in large part of a specific, precisely executed series of physical movements, my primary concern was to be as mechanically accurate a model for the new students as I could possibly be. This striving taught me a very valuable lesson: It helped me understand how to keep my consciousness in my movements. This focus of attention in the movements is central to the practice of Tai-Chi Chuan. However, when I had practiced before for my own sake, I was never as motivated to concentrate on my movements as when I became as a model. From the beginning of the semester, I paid closer attention than ever to how Simu executed the movements, and as I modeled them for the class and corrected the students' forms, I became more acutely aware of the finest details and nuances of each and every movement. Simply through this concentration of attention to detail, I learned as much or more about the movements as the students in the class did. Moreover, through this concentration I learned how to concentrate better. And I learned of the power of concentration; indeed concentration *is* power.

While I was learning the form, Simu once said, "You practice over the weekend. I can tell when you come back Monday if you practiced!" I learned how she could tell: It can easily be seen in the performance of a student. I also learned that I can accurately determine the degree of a student's motivation and determination to learn. Also, I can spot the "gifted" ones, the ones who "get it" from the beginning. I can see those who struggle but have the will to make marked improvement, those who have to struggle against weak self-motivation, and those who are in class for an easy grade or some other reason than a genuine desire to learn the art. Then there are those who not only "get it" physically, but get it spiritually as well.

Tai-Chi Chuan is a spiritual discipline as well as a mental-physical discipline—a discipline that can show one how the spiritual, the mental, and the physical are actually one, while seemingly separate. Simu's late husband, the Master Kuo Lien-Ying, said, [while practicing] "The whole concentration of the mind is ... on the spirit, ... " and I've learned to recognize the students who have caught hold of the Spirit and concentrate their minds on it. They are elevated above simply being students learning and earning college credit in a physical education class; they are students on a spiritual path.

I gained confidence in myself as a teacher during that semester. Simu commented frequently, "You're doing a good, job, but not a very good job." (Simu would never tell anyone she cares about that they are very good for fear that "the monster" will get them—the monster, I presume, being false ego that comes too frequently with praise and false pride.) I think she was right, not only because I thoroughly trust her, but because of the students' reaction to me. We would typically work with the class as a whole for the first half-hour, then allow the students to work individually or in small groups to practice as we circulated through the class, making ourselves available to make corrections, demonstrate movements, or answer questions. Several times I have stopped to demonstrate a move to two or three students and have attracted groups of students to work on that move. I have had individual students tell me I'm a good teacher. When Simu has heard that, she interrupts, "Not very good, though. He's OK, but not very good," she gleams and giggles, then scolds the student with a mock-fierce voice and a smile in her eyes: "You want the monster to get him?"

Teaching Tai-Chi Chuan is my bliss. I realized as I observed our classes practicing together *en masse* that I get a thrill, a kind of excited joy, actually, that can make me physically shiver when I see a student "getting it," catching hold of the Spirit. When I myself have hold of the Spirit, I ride it as if I were riding an animal, something alive, tangible, moving—something that moves with infinite strength, smoothness, and grace. I have eyes to see a student catch hold of the ride, and I have a heart that thrills at the sight. For these two things I am infinitely grateful; these are loose kin to the bliss I speak of, and these things together suggest strongly that I should be teaching Tai-Chi Chuan.

The bliss of Tai-Chi Chuan has brought great fullness to my life in ways that I never would have imagined. Now, with a Ph.D. in human development and working as a gerontologist in Portland, Oregon, I see *Yin-Yang in Tai-Chi Chuan and Daily Life* as the culmination of hard work and apprenticeship.

Preface

JONAS HAMILTON

In her previous monographs—*Long Life, Good Health through Tai-Chi Chuan* and *Shao-Lin Chuan: The Rhythm and Power of Tai-Chi*—Simu Kuo explained the two fundamental systems of exercise and self-defense (Tai-Chi Chuan and Shao-Lin Chuan) that she and her husband, Kuo Lien-Ying, brought to the United States in 1966. In this book she broadens her scope, teaching the philosophy underlying the martial arts of which she has been a distinguished teacher for nearly forty years. Her readers will soon appreciate that "Tai-Chi," for example, is not just exercise or self-defense *(Chuan)*, but a traditional philosophy, embracing every aspect of life. The common thread in Simu's writings is a desire to assist students and to enrich their practice—the same generosity of spirit that prompted Sifu Kuo and his wife to leave the security of China in order to bring this philosophical art to the San Francisco Bay Area. San Franciscans soon became accustomed to the sight of students practicing in the pre-dawn vapors of Portsmouth Square. In the last two years of his life, Sifu instructed Simu in the philosophical basis of Tai-Chi Chuan and Shao-Lin Chuan. By the time of his death in 1984, these teachings had become part of the curriculum at San Francisco State University, complementing the popular Tai-Chi Chuan and Shao-Lin Chuan classes. Thus, the seed of Tai-Chi Chuan and Shao-Lin Chuan—and of Confucius and Lao Tzu—has taken firm root and borne plentiful fruit. Following her husband's example, Simu Kuo refuses to rest on her laurels, and she continues to strive as a teacher and artist. She has researched the roots of Tai-Chi Chuan and Shao-Lin Chuan in frequent trips to China. The product of these investigations, Simu's new book is a great gift for those seeking to follow in her footsteps.

Anyone closely associated with Simu Kuo as a student becomes subject to her penetrating scrutiny. Naturally, one's posture and manner of performing the forms receive correction. The student may be surprised that this attention often extends to other apparently unrelated matters, such as dress or moral conduct. A careful reading of Simu Kuo's new book should make it clear that her method is based on traditional principles, carefully considered. Now the general public can enjoy the spirit of Simu Kuo's teaching: namely, her vision of our moral responsibility for each other. Tai-Chi Chuan has never been for Simu Kuo a selfish pursuit; she has always sought to foster not just balance, coordination, and good physical health, but also social harmony and proper conduct. Following Confucius (or Plato, or Aristotle), Simu Kuo believes that a healthy community depends on healthy individuals. In these pages the serious student will find inspiration. For others, Simu Kuo's book puts her magnificent art in its proper cultural and historical perspective.

Simmone Kuo with her husband, Kuo Lien-Ying, and their son, Chung-Mei Kuo

Acknowledgments

I would like to thank and acknowledge all of my good students of the past thirty-eight years.

Deep gratitude to the Chinese students whose generous contributions helped open the Lien-Ying Tai-Chi Chuan Academy in 1965.

Thanks to Dawson Lee and also to Wendy and Colin Hunter for their generous assistance over a period of three months in 1975 while I was developing a series of Tai-Chi Chuan educational programs for KPIX (Channel 5 in San Francisco, California).

Thanks to Professor Yao You-Wei (姚有爲) and Professor Jin Yu (金玉) of Yangzhou Teachers University for the painting used on the cover of this book.

And a special thanks to the Western students who have been willing to work with me and help with this book, continuing the Chinese cultural tradition of appreciation between student and teacher. For their help proofreading, editing, and rewriting this book, I express my thankfulness to Shannon Cook, Jeffrey Kessler, Tim McAuliffe, and Daniel Rybold.

Thanks, too, to Pam Suwinsky for her discerning editorial assistance, to Susan Quasha for her patience and skill in designing this book, and to all those at North Atlantic Books for their help with the production and publication processes.

This book is the culmination of the teaching from my classes at San Francisco State University and is a companion volume to *Long Life, Good Health through Tai-Chi Chuan*. I offer it as a gift to the new generation of Tai-Chi Chuan students.

Sheshe (Thank you).

PART 1

Simu's Teachings

I

Introduction to the Martial Arts Tradition

FIGURE I.1: *Simmone Kuo performs warm-up exercise called "Skating Lake."*

The History of Chinese Martial Arts

(In Chinese)

（一）太極拳之起源与发展

早在人類社會產生之初，我们的祖先为了生存，不得不断地与大自然，及大自然中的各類野獸進行博鬥。在博鬥中，他们由簡单地模仿野獸的攻守动作到進一步观察各類动物的攀登、跨越、跳躍动作象而形成了具有人類的風格的最初的拳禾。隨着朝代的变化，中國拳術這一偉大的文化也進一步发展改良，尤其是在中國的京劇、雜劇以及以後的少林寺立現後，更加促使中國拳進一步完善。太極拳正走借鑑了少林拳的精華，進而完善並最終发展为今天的，以增強体質，促進人的身心健康的体育活动。

The History of Chinese Martial Arts

The martial arts began as soon as there were people on Earth who struggled with animals and each other for food and territory. People started practicing martial arts thousands of years ago in China by studying nature and by observing and imitating the movements of animals in combat. The stillness of mountains, the fluidity of rivers, the constellations of stars, and the power, speed, and camouflage of animals inspired the development of the ancient martial arts.

Each region of China had its own distinct native style, the basic division being between North and South. These early practices were later collected and refined into schools of martial arts for self-defense and physical conditioning. Approximately three thousand years ago, the early Chinese martial artists began to group together their observations and developed sets, or forms, into numerous distinct schools and styles.

Chinese martial arts are referred to collectively in Chinese as *wu shu. Wu* means "martial," and *shu* means "arts," "skills," or "magic," in the sense that you must practice the art for a long time to attain the skill to make it seem like magic. The Chinese martial arts can be divided into two main schools: external and internal. The "outer" school emphasizes primarily physical development, while the "inner" school emphasizes mental development as well. The external forms are characterized by developing speed and muscular power, building up the physical body, concentrating on the bones and marrow, and stressing quick movements, leaps, and kicks. Some examples are Shao-Lin Chuan, Japanese karate, Korean taekwondo, and judo. The internal forms are characterized by slower, gentler movements, concentrating on the muscles and tendons for the development of internal energy. In the internal arts, it is the mind that is the prime mover. Some examples are Tai-Chi Chuan, Shing Yi, and Pa Kua.

The Life of a Martial Artist in the Olden Days
訣口藝賣

In the "olden" days—from the early days of the Ching Dynasty (ca. 1650 C.E.)—
the martial artist made his living by traveling from town to town doing martial arts
demonstrations for the local people. When he set up space for his performance,
he first had to respect the local martial artists by reciting an introduction and a
presentation of himself in a courteous and formal manner. The first thing he would
do is to praise the locality by proclaiming:

> This is the great land of the crouching tiger and hidden dragon.
> I am an old master with no crown on my head and my young
> student has no license atop his shoulders. You want to know who I
> am? After I finish, I will come to your schools and pay my respects
> to you. Right now I bow to you and your ancestors in greeting
> and great respect for you as to my oldest master. Please accept my
> courtesy now.

He would then bend his right knee and kneel on his left in a sign of humility so
that no one would challenge him. This was the code for martial artists. After the
demonstration, the martial artist would ask for a donation. He would say, "I would
like the street cleaners, shoemakers, jewelry makers, farmers, teachers, students,
businessmen, horse and buggy drivers, and any other workers to give a donation
after the demonstration. We will deeply appreciate this, because we need to pay for
our food and hotel." In this courteous way, the passion was ignited in the people for
the street artists, especially the martial artists.

The Life of a Martial Artist in the Olden Days

(In Chinese)

来到此地，大邦之地，龍藏臥虎之地，
老師父頭上沒寫王字，少師父背後沒掛招
牌，若要知道老師姓甚叫甚，回到登門
叩拜，不知老師父姓甚叫甚，當場叩拜作
揖，前謂長輩卑父老，左右謂兄才姐妹少
師父院皓了，師父時候不早了，人也不少，祇
說不練走，嘴把事，只辣不晚慢把事，
老師父說，好，辣，練完怎麼辦，少師父院，吃飯
要飯錢，佳店安庄錢，跟雅安呢，老師父說，跟所
有一切的工人都說去來等，少師父又同，如果今
天沒帶錢的怎麼辦，老師父說，沒閒係站着
助陣人多財旺，掌聲大些，就村，鑼鼓一敲，表演閙
始了，此以說，孔多人不惱，武術界的人就不會挑戰
你，然後就會知你做好兄弟，所以說，中國定自
古以來，礼義之邦的國家，这就叫，有理不在高原，
山高遮不了太陽，

The Courtesy of Martial Arts Street Performers in Olden Days

FIGURE I.2: *This is the land of Hidden Dragon and Crouching Tiger.*

FIGURE I.3: *Hidden Dragon*

FIGURE I.4: *Crouching Tiger*

The Legacy of Shao-Lin Temple

FIGURE I.5: *Monks and martial artists stand before the gate of Shao-Lin Temple.*

The foundation of the modern external forms of Chinese martial arts is Shao-Lin Chuan. *Shao* means "youthful," and *lin* means "forest." Shao-Lin Chuan is "the Fist of the Youthful Forest." It was developed by and named after the Buddhist monks of the Shao-Lin Temple, built in a youthful forest in the mountains of Hunan Province in northern China. In the sixth century C.E., an Indian monk named Bodhidharma (known in Chinese as Ta-Mo) visited the Shao-Lin monastery. He had journeyed from India to China as a pilgrim carrying scrolls of Buddhist *dharma* (teachings). Bodhidharma withdrew to the Shao-Lin Temple and took refuge in a cave outside the monastery to meditate. He noticed that the monks had physically degenerated from sitting so long in meditation, so he taught them a set of movements with which they could revive themselves. He taught them yogic stretching exercises from India, which they then incorporated into the native fighting forms of their youth.

At the temple lived a group of eighteen monks who had been a band of criminals before retreating to the temple in remorse. They were excellent martial artists but had always used their skill in fighting to intimidate and rob travelers. The eighteen monks adapted Bodhidharma's teachings ingeniously to the local people's fighting forms, refining the set of exercises into the Shao-Lin Chuan form that was passed down from generation to generation to the present. After their conversion to a virtuous way of life, these eighteen monks became so famous for their good deeds and public service that they came to be recognized in Chinese culture as *lohans*, heroic examples of the possibility for redirecting chaotic and violent energy toward inner development and the common good.

Before the Shao-Lin Temple period (sixth century C.E.), Chinese fighting forms were wild in nature, tending toward violence and purely pragmatic application for battle. Through the compassionate influence of Buddhism, Chinese martial arts became a philosophically based system oriented toward health, exercise, and inner development. The martial arts tradition of China is like a great tree with many branches, the trunk and roots of which have grown from the rich soil of Shao-Lin Temple. It was here that the numerous and varied native fighting forms of China were refined into a system that has thrived for fifteen hundred years. The refinements that occurred at Shao-Lin Temple have been rich in long-lasting benefits, and the temple is honored as the source of the distinctive Chinese martial arts tradition. Other traditional Chinese arts, such as Beijing opera and acrobatics, have also been influenced and regularly include martial arts training for their performers. More important, the martial arts tradition conceived at Shao-Lin Temple has provided valuable resources for personal health and development to countless generations in China and throughout the world.

FIGURE I.6: *Shao-Lin Temple Village student group practices near the Pagoda Forest, May 2001.*

FIGURE I.7: *Simmone Kuo performs line 3 of the ten-line Shao-Lin form known as Tan-Tui, or "Springy Legs."*

The History of the 64-Movement Tai-Chi Chuan Set

(In Chinese)

六十四式太極拳傳授史

武林高手張三豐曾習武于武當山，在武當期間，虔修苦練，潛心鑽研創立了六十四式太極拳，武當由此而出名。

中國武林門派衆多，拳術雖精却非其門人不傳，所以江湖上對六十四式太極拳也祇是可慕不可及，會此拳種的人更是寥寥無幾。

邯鄲境内的永年縣，有個武術之鄉广府城，是楊氏太極拳的創始人楊禄禪的故鄉，楊禄禪的次子楊鈺，字班侯（一八三七～一八九二），自幼隨父學武，練就一身好功夫，他不但繼承了楊家的拳術，而且還幾經展轉練就了張三豐的六十四式太極拳，成年應召進京後，又慧眼識金收了尊師敬拳的愛徒王喬宇，王專攻六十四式，經多年勤練，終得張三豐拳術真諦。北平和平門内昌祖廟主持見王喬宇拳術高超，就讓出廟内空地讓其傳授武功。

當時的中國正值軍閥混戰，許多青年人在探尋着救國之道。有一位叫郭連蔭的青年武功高强，爲進一步提高自己的造詣報效祖國，慕名前去拜訪王喬宇。王見郭才貌出衆，功底扎實，聰慧過人，便決定將六十四式傳給他，從此王、郭即是師徒，又是拳友，二人還盟約將六十四式太極拳完整無變地傳下去，意在弘揚中華拳術之精髓。到五十年代初，郭連蔭滿懷對武術的熱愛之情，肩負歷史賦予的責任，途經香港，來到中國的台灣省—寶島。到臺後，他勤奮習武、研磨拳道、光大拳術。著名書畫家于右任先生觀其武、賞其德，鼓勵郭著書。郭便于一九六○年完成了他的第一部作品《太極拳譜》，于右任親自爲其封面提字。

中華文化學院院長黄文山先生讀了郭連蔭的《太極拳譜》後深受啓發，于一九六五年邀請郭連蔭到美國西岸表演、講授武功，郭所到之處均受到當地人士的歡迎和賞許，隨後在舊金山創立了「連蔭太極學院」。金山省立大學體育系還把原版六十四式太極拳定爲學生的必修課。

現任連蔭太極學院院長盧澄茹女士是郭連蔭大師的夫人兼弟子，被金山省立大學聘爲太極拳教授。爲把這套古老的拳術完好無損地流傳于世，盧女士深感責任重大，借籌此書機會，二○○一年七月親自到中國河北邯鄲尋訪太極名師楊班侯的故鄉，與楊氏傳人當面切磋，交流武功。

顧太極之花在大洋兩岸盛開！顧這套古老的拳術永遠爲人類的健康和文明做出貢獻！

The History of the 64-Movement Tai-Chi Chuan Set

Tai-Chi Chuan, an internal martial art form, incorporates aspects of Shao-Lin Chuan. Shao-Lin Chuan forms the basis for all martial arts, and should be learned first whenever possible.

Tai, in Chinese, means "vast and all-encompassing," while *Chi* is the "ultimate or extreme point." The Tai-Chi concept existed long before the creation of Tai-Chi Chuan, influencing early Chinese philosophy, medicine, and religion. The martial art of Tai-Chi Chuan is "the Fist of Balance." In Tai Chi Chuan, the emphasis has been not on physical strength and muscular power, but on building up internal energy, developing mental concentration, and the coordination of natural breathing with movement.

FIGURE I.7: *Chang San-Feng, the founder of Tai-Chi Chuan. Based on the rubbing taken from a stone engraving at the Monastery of Hsun Tien on Wu Tang Mountain, Hubei Province, China.*

The creation of Tai-Chi Chuan is attributed to the legendary Chang San-Feng. He left no historical record. Legend has it that he studied outer schools of martial arts in his youth and was a well-known bodyguard of the Sung Dynasty emperors in the eleventh century C.E. He met a Taoist with whom he practiced for many years and whom he accompanied to Wu Tang Mountain in Hubei Province. Here he united many Taoist martial arts—such as Pa Kua and Shing Yi—with Shao-Lin Chuan and Tai-Chi philosophy to create Tai-Chi Chuan. There are many stories of how he came up with the form. Some claim it came to him in a dream. Others say he was visited and taught the form by a powerful spirit. Some say he developed it through intense study of the *I Ching*. But the most common story is that he came up with the idea after his many years of martial arts training and Taoist studies while watching a snake and a crane fight on Wu Tang Mountain.

Wu Tang Mountain

China contains a great many wonderful mountains. Among these are Five Sacred Taoist Mountains where Taoist philosophers lived as hermits in inaccessible regions in order to cultivate the elixir of life. Wu Tang in Hubei is one of these. These mountains are the birthplace of the 64-movement Tai-Chi form, created here by Chang San-Feng to benefit the world.

FIGURE I.8: *Simmone Kuo stands before the three peaks known as "The Three Old Men" atop Wu Tang Mountain.*

單鞭

軸－太極一詞最早見於《易經》：「太極謂天地未分之前，元氣混而為一，即太初、太乙也。」十三勢作為太極拳別名的由來即五種基本步法和八種基本手法，俗稱『五步八門』，即五行與八掛相合而成。腰力運用得當，能確保全身平衡，有助內勁運轉，所以太極拳走架過程中必須以腰為軸。腰為腎之本，人生三寶為精、氣、神，命門為水火之府，陰陽之宅，精氣之海，生死之實，是元氣之根，所以練拳轉換變勢時要『命意源頭在腰際，刻刻留心在腰間。』

靜－太極拳術重用意，腰如車軸心行氣，靜字為首，頭腦冷靜，心寧膽定，全神貫注，以意運身，動中求靜，靜而能得氣，得氣則通過，病灶通則不痛。

FIGURE I.9: *Chang San-Feng on Wu Tang Mountain, with students behind him practicing Tai-Chi Chuan's Single Whip.*

Although the 64-movement Tai-Chi Chuan form was famous in China, not many people could execute this style because instructions were only given to the students of the Wu Tang School. The first time it is formally documented is in the "Tai-Chi Chuan Dictionary" of Wang Tsung-Yue, and later in the sixteenth-century writings of the Chen family. The Chens kept this practice in their family from generation to generation, only allowing two individuals from outside the family to learn this style. One of these was Yang Ban-Ho, who mastered the style in the nineteenth century, then moved to Beijing and opened a school to teach Tai-Chi Chuan to the royalty and the common people there. Yang took on a dedicated student named Wang Chou-Yee, who was very diligent and closely practiced his teacher's style, careful to preserve Yang's teachings without any changes. From Yang Ban-Ho and his famous disciple Wang Chou-Yee comes the Tai-Chi Chuan form as we know it today. In his old age Wang lived in the Li Tsu Temple in the Ho-ping Gate sector of Beijing. Many students came to him in the front yard of the temple during the early twentieth century. Among these was Kuo Lien-Ying.

FIGURE I.10: *Dedication to Wang Chou-Yee*

FIGURE I.11: *Grandmaster Yang Ban-Ho*

FIGURE I.12: *Kuo Lien-Ying*

The Life of Grand Master Kuo Lien-Ying

FIGURE I.13: *Sifu Kuo performs a double kick*

Kuo Lien-Ying studied various martial arts from the time he was twelve years old. He was eager to improve his skills to better serve his country, which was in a time of turmoil. When he heard of Wang's mastery he went to visit him in Beijing. Acknowledging Kuo as an outstanding and intelligent young man with a solid foundation in martial arts, Wang decided to teach him the 64-movement form of Tai-Chi Chuan. Beyond their teacher-student relationship, the two became good friends and pledged to each other that they would pass on the 64-movement form to later generations. They vowed not to change any aspect of the set, so that the lineage would remain pure and the best of the Chinese martial arts would not be lost.

Kuo, who had served as a congressman to the National Assembly of China, left his homeland in 1952, traveled through Hong Kong, and settled in the Chinese province of Taiwan for fourteen years. In Taiwan he researched and wrote about Tai-Chi Chuan while teaching martial arts part-time. In 1965, at the invitation of Huang Wen Shan, Dean of the Chinese Culture Institute, he sailed to the United States. In San Francisco's Chinatown he founded with his wife the Lien-Ying Tai-Chi Chuan Academy. Sifu Kuo was very well received by the local people, and the studio has flourished ever since.

The Lien-Ying Tai-Chi Chuan Academy

The master of the Lien Ying Tai-Chi Chuan Academy is now Simmone Kuo, wife and student of Kuo Lien-Ying. Simu Kuo (Lu Eing-Ru) left Taiwan in 1966 and came to the United States with her husband. She studied Tai-Chi Chuan, Shao-Lin Chuan, Shao-Lin Staff, Shao-Lin Sword, Tai-Chi Sword, Pa Kua, and Shing Yi with her husband. The form that is presented in her books and classes carries the same vow she made to Master Kuo not to change any aspect of the traditional form. In gratitude for the selflessness of the three masters of Yang, Wang, and Kuo, Simmone Kuo paid a special visit to Han Dan, the birthplace of Yang Ban Ho, in July 2001 and exchanged ideas with students of the Yang family school.

FIGURE I.14: *Kuo family studio in Chinatown, San Francisco, on Portsmouth Square. Established in 1965, it moved to its current location in 1989.*

The Kuo Lien-Ying Family

FIGURE I.15: *Father and son play at the Monkey Form.*

FIGURE I.16: *On a cold winter day in December 1993, Simu visited Sifu's ashes in Hu Ho Hao Te, Inner Mongolia. In the "Green Grass Cemetery" rest heroes such as Sifu, who was honored with a state funeral, and whose remains rest peacefully in this small wooden treasure box.*

II

Yin-Yang in Theory

Tai-Chi Philosophy

(In Chinese)

太極拳之哲學

根据中国古代的論理学,太極拳是武術,太極是哲学。

太極,太是指廣潤無邊,大的意思,極是高峯無頂之

意,古代哲学家伏羲最初認為宇宙是空虛無止境的,

並把這一状態称为無極。根據這一学説,進而推斷在

虛無的宇宙之外,存在两了主要力量,陰与"陽",或者

説是"正"与"負"。中國人统称陰陽为太極。並認為極其

是永恆的存在萬物之中的,這其中已括大自然的氣候,

植物,時辰,地壤,以及现代的科学研究与陰陽有関。

但是陰与陽不可截迷分開,独立存在.在運动中的者

紧密联系，相互转换，相辅相成，协调配合成宇宙

向乃至人的一系列活动。简述之，白昼为阳，黑夜为

阴，动为阳，静为阴。太极拳正是以这一学说为基础，

主张不要过分用力，要体现人的本质的统一，发挥体内的

能量，协调阴阳两力。因此，在练太极拳时，速度要

适中，不快不慢，刚柔结合，使动作柔和而又连贯。

功夫与武术

功夫是中国武学的一种通俗称呼。正统的说法应该

是武术。功夫一词照字面解释是「时间」，练习用来

誓惕那些习武之人是需要时间来练习，并非一朝一夕

可成功的。

The Tao

Tao is an ancient Chinese concept loosely translated in English as "the Way," or "the path." The "way" of the Tao is not static, but a constantly changing, continually ongoing process. It is "the way" of all things, the "way" all is created, the many ways things evolve, and the way it all eventually ends. All phenomena in this world of change and transformation are seen as dynamically interrelated, and supported, by the matrix of the Tao, which underlies the entire universe. From this fabric, all things are issued forth and interact.

It is said that "the Tao gives rise to all forms, yet it has no form of it's own …" (Lao Tzu, *Tao Te Ching*). It is also written that "in Tao's changes and hidden permutations … Heaven and earth and the ten thousand things were issued forth and are still inseparable from the Tao" (Lao Tzu, *Hua Hu Ching*).

FIGURE II.1: *The author's mother holds prayer beads.*

From Wu-Chi to Tai-Chi

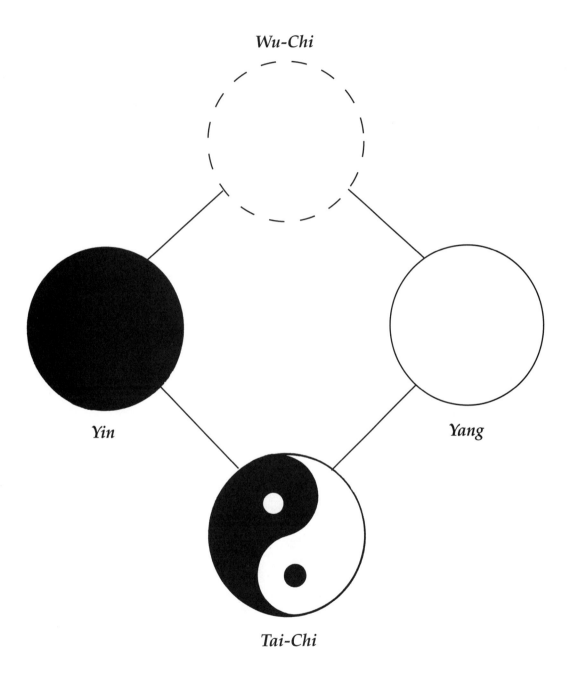

FIGURE II.2: *From Wu-Chi to Tai-Chi*

According to Tai-Chi philosophy, before this universe came into being there was nothing but a formless, boundless Void. Chinese philosophers termed this state *Wu-Chi,* meaning "no limit" (represented in FIGURE II.2 by a dotted circle). In the limitless emptiness, polarization occurred and the primordial energetic charges spontaneously distinguished themselves. The duality of complementary opposites is known by the Chinese characters *Yin* and *Yang.* (In FIGURE II.2, Yang is represented by the light circle, and Yin is represented by the dark circle.) These two primal opposite forces were irresistibly attracted to each other and combined to form complementary halves of a singularity, containing all the energy of our universe fused into one point, the seed of all manifestation. This state of unity, known as *Tai-Chi,* is represented by the classic symbol shown in FIGURE II.3.

YIN   **YANG**

FIGURE II.3: *Tai-Chi symbol*

Tai-Chi symbolizes the whole of which all things are a part. "Tai-Chi" is made up of two Chinese characters: *Tai*, meaning large and all-encompassing, and *Chi*, meaning ultimate or extreme point. Simply stated, *Tai-Chi* refers to the "absolute" or "ultimate point" of the universe, which is at once everywhere and nowhere in particular, forever constant and existing in all things. Tai-Chi is the union and dynamic balancing of the primal forces of Yin and Yang, through whose interplay the cosmos comes into being. These forces are balanced perfectly in Tai-Chi, the state in which Yin and Yang are fused together, but once they begin differentiating themselves they set in motion the continual process of evolution, leading to the arising of all phenomena. Within the expansive Oneness, top began to separate from bottom, up came to be distinguished from down, centrifugal and centripetal forces began to push and pull, always seeking balance.

TAI   **CHI**

INFINITELY HORIZONTAL   INFINITELY VERTICAL

FIGURE II.4: *Tai-Chi means "balance," as is reflected in the translation of the Chinese root words, tai and chi, as "infinitely horizontal" and "infinitely vertical."*

Yin and Yang

The circle that represents the whole (Tai-Chi) is divided into Yin (black) and Yang (white) halves—two polar complements in harmonious balance. The two smaller circles in the centers (the eyes), shaded in the opposite color, illustrate that within Yin there is Yang, and vice versa (see FIGURE II.3). Yin and Yang contain within themselves, at their very centers, the seeds of change. The curve dividing them indicates that this change is dynamic and continuous. Each half invades the other half and establishes itself in the center of its opposite.

Every whole "thing"—from a tree to a person to a business, an atom, planet, or universe—can be seen as a metaphorical Tai-Chi, with corresponding Yin and Yang aspects. Once Yin and Yang are distinguished, each one can also be seen as a whole and broken down further into its own integral Yin and Yang parts. We can see this creative process unfold all around us. The universal process of Being arising from Non-Being through the fusion of opposites, followed by the differentiation and increase of complexity from oneness to myriad forms, can be observed in the studies of modern cosmology, the evolution of species, the conception and development of individuals, and the arising of ideas.

Here is a deeper explanation of how Yin and Yang both originated from and provide for the origin of life:

T'AI-CHI
（太極）

"Chinese philosophers speak of the origin of all created things under the name of *T'ai-chi*. This is represented in their books by a figure, which is thus formed: On the semi-diameter of a given circle describe a semi-circle, and on the remaining semi-diameter, but on the other side, describe another semi-circle.  The whole figure represents the *T'ai-chi*, and the two divided portions, formed by the curved line, typify what are called the Yin（陰）and the *Yang*（陽）, in respect to which, this Chinese mystery bears a singular parallel to that extraordinary fiction of Egyptian mythology, the supposed intervention of a masculo-feminine principle in the development of the mundane egg. The *T'ai-chi* is said to have produced the Yang and the Yin, the active and passive, or male and female principle, and these last to have produced all things.[1] The circle represents the origin of all created things, and when split up into two segments, it is said to be reduced to its primary constituents, the male and female principles.

The T'ai-chi is said to be the essence of extreme virtue and perfection in heaven and earth, men and things. Speaking figuratively it is like the ridge-pole [sic] of a house, or the central pillar of a granary, being always in the middle of the building, and the whole structure on every side depends upon it for support.

From the T'ai-chi, which may be called the Great Extreme or Ultimate Principle, composed of the YIN AND YANG (q.v.), springs the FIVE ELEMENTS (q.v.), which are the source of all things, and man, having been evolved from the union of the male and female principles, is enriched at his birth by the possession of the Five Virtues（五常）, viz: Benevolence（仁）; Purity（義）; Propriety（禮）; Wisdom（智）; and Truth（信）.

The *T'ai-chi* surrounded by the EIGHT DIAGRAMS *(q.v.),* is a common design of good omen, and is frequently painted above the doors of Chinese houses as a charm against evil influences (*vide* EIGHT DIAGRAMS, YIN AND YANG).

---

[1] AUTHORITY.
Davis: The Chinese, Vol. II, p. 62

Source: C. A. S. Williams, Outline of Chinese Symbolism and Art Motifs. *New York: Dover Publications, Inc., 1976.*

Fu Hsi
(In Chinese)

伏羲

史料記載，"三皇"伏羲、神衣、軒轅、是人類始祖，特別是伏羲，他智慧超人與眾不同，他經常留意觀察、分析研究各種自然現象，發明了烤炙、蒸煮、教會人們食的習慣並利用光影創造了陰陽、四象、五行、八卦這套符号，幫助人們認識自然災害苍萌生的部份規律和避開這自然災害的危害。世界人類的"開天明道"都是伏羲的功德和貢献。

Fu Hsi
伏羲

Fu Hsi was born in the twenty-eighth century B.C.E. (2953–2832 B.C.E.) in the city of Tian-Shui, in China's Gansu Province. He was the first of the three emperors of the pre-historical period of China, and he is considered the mythological- legendary grandfather of Chinese culture. Through his meditations on the workings of nature, he is said to have learned and taught the ancient Chinese people how to use fire and tools, hunt, cook, write, practice medicine, play music, and more. He is also credited with developing the theory of Yin and Yang, which became the fundamental concept underlying Chinese philosophy and natural science.

甘肅省, 天水市

FIGURE II.5: *Depicted on the wall of a temple dedicated to him in Tian Shui in the Gansu Province, Emperor Fu Hsi sits atop the mountain and observes the cycles of nature in the universe. He is the father of Tai-Chi philosophy and Yin-Yang theory.*

Reflecting deeply on the natural world, Fu Hsi perceived the harmonious relationship in all things. He understood that this harmony was due to the two opposite forces of Yin and Yang complementing and transmuting into each other. Fu Hsi envisioned the cosmos as an ongoing process of change, in which phenomena arise from and return to the Void. He observed the day followed by night, the waxing and waning of the moon, the cycling of seasons, and revolutions of celestial bodies; and he understood that the same universal laws govern creation at every level. He realized that all the universe is the unfolding of a single event and all creatures are transient forms, each a unique and shifting blend of Yin and Yang, substance and essence. He saw the world around him as the interplay of these Yin and Yang energies and developed a system to record his observations.

Fu Hsi used two simple characters to symbolize Yin and Yang: solid — (Yang), and broken – – (Yin) lines. Yang is division brought together in union (two-in-one), which eventually divides again to become Yin (one-in-two). He is said to have taken the form of the notation from the markings on the back of a tortoise, which in Chinese mythology is a symbol of immortality. Fu Hsi's ideas form the foundation for Tai-Chi philosophy, and his notation allows for explorations into deeper levels of complexity, preserved in ancient classics of Chinese philosophy.

Interplay of Yin and Yang

The foundation principles of Tai-Chi philosophy are the balance of opposing but complementary forces—Yin and Yang; the concept of "polar reversal," which allows Yin to transform into Yang once it reaches its peak and vice versa; and the process of continuous change between the two extremes.

All things have two aspects, or sides—a Yin side and Yang side. Yin and Yang can be distinguished, but they cannot be separated. They depend on each other for definition. Yin-Yang theory asserts that a part can only be understood in its relation to the whole. No entity can ever be isolated from its relationship to other entities; no thing can exist in and of itself. Nothing is completely Yin or completely Yang. Phenomena are said to represent one or the other in relation to something else.

TABLE II.1 shows some ways that we can experience these polarities interacting around us.

TABLE II.1: **Properties of Yin and Yang**

Yin (– –)			Yang (—)		
passive			active		
feminine			masculine		
night	intuition	moon	day	intellect	sun
winter	west		summer	east	
	low	essence		high	substance
hidden	wetness	bones	manifest	dryness	skin
	midnight	sides		noon	corners
	empty	material		full	immaterial
dense	right			left	
heavy		interior body	light		exterior body
receptive	hollow			solid	day
external		space	internal		time
earth	cold		heaven	hot	
dark	inhaling	gravity		exhaling	electro-
down			up		magnetism

We must remember that these classifications are not permanent, but are only relevant in relation to their opposite. The dualities change in relation to each other. For example, the Earth is Yin when compared to the sun (the Earth revolves around the sun), but Yang when compared with the moon (the moon revolves around the Earth); the proton holds the central, Yang position in the atom as compared to the electron orbiting in the peripheral, Yin position; but the electron functions as the active, Yang aspect of the atom in chemical reactions as compared with the passive, Yin functions of the proton.

All things/wholes/Tai-Chis have both Yin and Yang aspects, and any individual characteristic of Yin or Yang can be further subdivided into Yin and Yang. This is an extension of the logic that divides all phenomena into Yin and Yang. Each aspect, once distinguished, can be recognized as a Tai-Chi whole, thus allowing further division within any element of Yin or Yang. For example, in the dichotomy of cold (Yin) and hot (Yang), cold (Yin) can be further divided into icy cold (more Yin) and cool (more Yang), and hot (Yang) can be divided into fiery hot (more Yang) and warm (more Yin).

As shown in the Tai-Chi symbol, each opposing side contains at its center the seed of its opposite, and as either force climaxes it begins the polar reversal transformation into its complementary aspect. Just as at the peak of the day, noon, the sun begins to set into night, and after the shortest day of the year, at the winter solstice, the days begin to get longer. After a deep breath we need to exhale, and after holding our breath for a while we are compelled to take in air. After extensive activity, rest is needed, and after a good night's sleep we wake full of energy. Yin and Yang transform into each other once they reach their respective peaks, mutually creating each other.

There are many types of transformations: changes that occur harmoniously, the sudden ruptures characteristic of an extremely disharmonious situation, and various states of balance and imbalance in between. Gradual transformations occur smoothly, maintaining a proper, healthy balance of Yin and Yang. Transformation is thus seen as the source of all change in the universe. And neither is it always a slow or gradual process. In a relationship in which Yin and Yang are unbalanced for prolonged periods of time or in an extreme manner, the resulting transformations may be quite drastic, resulting in the transformation into opposites or the cessation of existence. For example, if we do not have rest and nourishment after periods of activity and exertion, we can become run down, sick, and may, in extreme cases, pass away. In this way Yin and Yang exert mutual control over each other. If Yin is excessive, then Yang will be weak, and vice versa.

Thus Yin and Yang continually create each other, control each other, and subtly transform into each other, unfolding through a kind of spontaneous cooperation, an inner dynamic in the nature of things. Harmony is a state in which the proportions of Yin and Yang are relatively balanced; disharmony occurs when there is imbalance. A deficiency of one aspect implies an excess of the other. Extreme disharmony occurs when the deficiency of one aspect cannot continue to support the excess of the other aspect. The resulting change may be a rebalancing or, if that is not possible, transformation into opposites. If this is also not possible, prolonged disharmony will ultimately lead to the cessation of existence.

All phenomena—from the most ordinary to the most exalted and abstract—can be described in their interactions and development through the system of Tai-Chi philosophy. The measuring of time and seasons, the combining of different foods, the proper use of land for agriculture and building, the effects of music, the care of the body, all the sciences of ancient China were understood in terms of the balancing of Yin and Yang energies and their transformations.

Chi

Chi can be defined as air, energy, life force, or subtle breath. It is the primary, underlying matrix of energy that connects and maintains all things, and from which all things spring forth. It is the invisible, omnipresent Yang energy in contrast to the tangible, local Yin matter that it transforms into, as suggested by the famous equation $E = mc^2$.

Various manifestations of this universal life energy are found in all living things, functioning in many ways. It manifests in human beings, as Prenatal or Postnatal Chi.

The first type of Chi originates before childbirth, the other is created and developed after birth. The fundamental source is Prenatal Chi, also called the Original or True Chi, which is transmitted by parents to their children at conception, and which is partly responsible for an individual's inherited constitution. Original Chi is stored in the kidneys but permeates the entire body. It is not only the source of all movement in the body, accompanying all movement, but it is also the source of harmonious transformation, protection, and warmness for the body. In addition to that, it governs retention of the body's substances and organs holding everything together. It secures organs in their proper place, keeps the blood moving in the veins, and prevents excessive loss of various bodily fluids, such as sweat and saliva, in order to ensure healthy physiological activity and development.

Postnatal Chi can be divided into two types: Air Chi and Earth Chi. After birth and throughout life, the Original Chi combines with Air Chi (the energy of the atmosphere), which is breathed in and extracted from the natural air in the environment by the lungs, and Earth Chi (the energy stored in the land, water, plants, and animals) is derived from the digestion of food and water. Breathing and eating link our Chi with the Chi of the universe. By taking this environmental Chi inside and combining it with Original Chi, we are able to harmonize with our surroundings. This is one reason Tai-Chi philosophy emphasizes proper diet and natural breathing.

Chi travels along invisible circuits in the body called *meridians*. The twelve major meridians, with several other "curious" meridians, flow throughout the body in skin, organs, and limbs alike. Just as blood is pumped through the body in the veins and arteries, and nervous system messages move throughout the body along the nerves, the meridians are the respective paths of Chi. In the human, intention directs Chi flow, and Chi moves the blood. The meridians are the invisible, active Yang complement of the material, passive Yin blood.

Chi, moves through the body in fixed and regular patterns. For example, both Lung-Chi and Stomach-Chi normally flow downward. On the other hand, both Spleen-Chi and Kidney-Chi should move upward. If this does not happen, there is an imbalance, which can lead to disease in the individual. If Lung-Chi moves upward, it causes coughing or difficulty in breathing. If Stomach-Chi moves upward, vomiting or some manner of throwing "up" occurs. If the Spleen-Chi goes down, it causes a prolapsed uterus, rectal difficulty, or morning diarrhea.

The Five Elemental Phases

Once distinguished within the wholeness of Tai-Chi, the two primal forces, Yin and Yang, begin to interact with each other and combine in various ways, passing through five elemental phases—symbolized by wood, fire, earth, metal, and water. These elemental phases are energy states that entities embody as they pass from Yin to Yang. After Yin and Yang distinguish time and space, the five elements define the seasons and the five directions. Once Yin and Yang determine life and death, and day and night, the five elemental phases describe the stages of the life cycle and the hours of the day. Anything described in terms of Yin and Yang can be further differentiated into its elemental phase, and each of these stages can also be distinguished as Yin or Yang in relation to the others.

The five elements interact with one another bringing forth and controlling each other in turn.

The sequence of their creation is:

  Wood creates fire

  Fire creates earth

  Earth creates metal

  Metal creates water

  Water creates wood

The sequence of control is:

  Wood controls earth

  Earth controls water

  Water controls fire

  Fire controls metal

  Metal controls wood

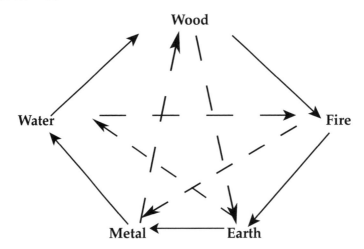

FIGURE II.6: *The five elemental phases' cycle of creation and control*

For example, the earthly mantle of our planet is created from the fires in its center and metal ore is formed within this earth. Water nourishes and gives life to plants, and their wood in turn provides the fuel for fire. On the other hand, water extinguishes fire, earthen dams control water, and metal axes chop down trees. We can see the way that the five elements manifest in the world around us in the following tables.

Source: Dianene M. Conelly, Traditional Acupuncture: The Law of the Five Elements. *Columbia, MD, Center for Traditional Acupuncture, Inc., 1975.*

TABLE II.2: Properties of the Five Elements

	Part of Body Governed	External Physical Manifestation	Power Granted	Smell	Climate
Wood	Sinews/ tendons	Nails, hands, feet	Capacity for control	Rancid	Wind
Fire	Blood vessels	Complexion	Capacity for joy and laughter	Scorched	Heat
Earth	Muscles and limbs	Flesh	Belching	Fragrant	Dampness, humidity
Metal	Skin, body hair	Skin, body care	Coughing	Rank	Dryness
Water	Bones, bone marrow	Head/hair	Trembling	Rotten	Winter rain

	Flavor	Orifice	Sense Organ	Emotion	Sound
Wood	Sour	Eyes	Eyes	Anger	Shouting
Fire	Bitter	Ears	Tongue	Joy, happiness	Laughing
Earth	Sweet	Mouth and lips	Mouth	Sympathy	Singing
Metal	Pungent, spicy	Nose	Nose	Grief	Weeping
Water	Salty	Genitals, urethra, anus	Ear	Fear	Groaning

	Storing of a Life	Dreams	Grain	Fruit
Wood	Spiritual faculties	Energy exhausted: Mushrooms lying under a tree not daring to get up. Energy deficient: Trees in mountain forest	Wheat	Peach
Fire	The spirit	Imbalance: Looking for fire, blazes full of abundant energy— one easily laughs or is afraid	Glutinous millet	Plum
Earth	Ideas and opinions	Lack of food and drink, putting up buildings or walls, chanting, playing music, heavy body, difficulty in rising	Millet	Apricot
Metal	Inferior, animal spirit	White objects, cruel killing of people, being frightened	Rice	Chestnut
Water	Willpower, ambition	Ships, boats, drowning people, lying in water and being frightened	Beans, peas	Dates

	Color	Season	Organs	Time of Day	Direction
Wood	Green	Spring	Liver, gall bladder	gb: 11 P.M.–1 A.M.; liv 1 A.M–3 A.M.	East
Fire	Red	Summer	Heart, small intestines	h: 11 A.M.–1 P.M.; si: 1–3 P.M.; circulation sex: 7–9 P.M.; three-heater: 9–11 P.M.	South
Earth	Yellow	Late summer	Spleen, stomach	st: 7–9 A.M.; sp: 9–11 A.M.	Center
Metal	White	Autumn	Lungs, large intestines	l: 3–5 A.M.; li: 5–7 A.M.	West
Water	Black	Winter	Kidneys, bladder	k: 5–7 P.M.; b: 3–5 P.M.	North

	Meat	Vegetable	Number	Musical Notes	Fluid Secretion
Wood	Chicken/ fowl	Mallow	8	"Chio" (sound of lute)	Bile
Fire	Mutton	Coarse grains	7	"Chih" (sound of 36-reed organ)	Sweat
Earth	Beef	Scallions	5	"Kung" (sound of drum)	Saliva
Metal	Horse	Onions	9	"Shang"	Mucous
Water	Pig (also scaley animals —fish)	Leeks	6	"Yu" (sound of 25-stringed lute)	Urine

Five Elements in Correspondence

With the Five Vital Organ Systems

METAL=LUNG

金 = 肺

WOOD-LIVER

木 = 肝

WATER=KIDNEY

水 = 腎

FIRE=HEART

火 = 心

EARTH=SPLEEN

土 = 脾

With the Five Tastes

METAL=SPICY

金 = 辣

WOOD=SOUR

木 = 酸

WATER=SALTY

水 = 醎

FIRE=BITTER

火 = 苦

EARTH=SWEET

土 = 甜

FIGURE II.7: *The five elements and the five senses of taste*

Chinese Medicine and Health Practices

As the tables suggest, the elemental energies manifest within the human body in many ways. Chinese medicine is based on harmonizing these energies to bring about a state of wholeness, total health, and complete wellness of being.

Chinese medical science is several thousands of years old, a systematized experience of the Chinese people living in and confronting the challenges of their natural environment. Chinese medical theory and practice are based upon Yin-Yang Theory and the Five Elemental Phases. When explaining the organization and structure of the human body, it recognizes that the upper body is Yang and the lower body is Yin; the surface of the body is Yang while the interior of the body is Yin; the back of the body is Yang and the abdominal area is Yin. The five elements manifest in the body as organ systems, which each have a Yin and Yang aspect. The Yin organs are solid. They produce and regulate the body's essential substances. The Yang organs are hollow. They metabolize and absorb into the body what the Yin organs need to create the fundamental substances then discard the excess. Yang organs bring in and transport, while Yin organs produce and store.

Chinese medicine recognizes five Yin organs (Heart, Liver, Spleen, Lungs, and Kidneys) and five Yang organs (the Gall Bladder, Stomach, Large Intestine, Small Intestine, and Bladder). The organ systems are named for their Yin organ.

TABLE II.3: **The Element–Organ Correlation**

Element	Yin Organ	Yang Organ
Fire	Heart	Small intestine
Earth	Spleen	Stomach
Metal	Lungs	Large intestine
Water	Kidneys	Bladder
Wood	Liver	Gall bladder

In the physiological sense, healthy and normal functional activities of the human body are the direct result of the harmonious relationship between opposition and balance. Traditional Chinese medicine is a preventative system. The traditional Chinese doctor would be paid by a family to make routine check-ups and keep them healthy. If someone in the family became ill, the doctor would have to do everything in his power to make them well again, and would not be paid again until he had done so.

46

Through diet, herbs, acupuncture, meditation, and exercises such as Tai-Chi Chuan, Chinese medicine seeks to bring about a condition of health that is not just the absence of disease, but an enhancement of well-being. This state of health is understood as a harmonious and dynamic balance of the various facets of human experience: somatic, psychological, and spiritual.

Yin-Yang and Time

The respective climaxes of Yin and Yang simultaneously affect opposite sides of the Earth. When it is noon in one area, on the other side of the planet it is midnight. When it is winter in the Northern Hemisphere, it is summer in the Southern Hemisphere, and vice versa.

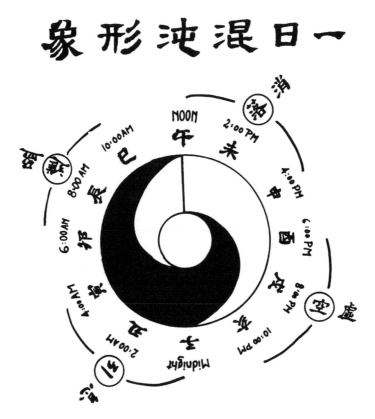

FIGURE II.8: *Chinese sundial*

A Day

Yin and Yang climax and transform gradually during the twenty-four-hour rotation of the Earth around its axis. Day, with the bright sunshine and most activity, is more Yang. Noon is when Yang is at its peak, after which it begins to transform through dusk to night, which is more Yin. Midnight is the climax of Yin, before it begins to wane toward dawn and day. During the hours of the day there is a balance of Yin-Yang as time passes.

FIGURE II.9: *Chinese moondial*

A Month

Yin and Yang energies also each climax and transform during the month-long cycle of the moon's revolution around the Earth. The white section of FIGURE II.9 represents the moon from the first to the thirtieth day of the monthly cycle. The thickness of Yin (black) versus Yang (white) corresponds to the changing cycles/proportions of light to dark (Yin to Yang) during the waxing and waning moon. The full moon is when Yin is at its peak, and the new moon is at the climax of Yang.

The Revolution of the Moon and Its Effects on the Human Body

月球圓缺與人體關係

宋代文豪蘇東坡的「人有悲歡離合，月有陰晴圓缺」佳句巧妙地說明了月亮的圓缺對人的心態、情緒的影響。當今科學界已通過天文物理、生物磁場方面的研究，證明了月亮變化對人體健康、人的情緒有着密切關係。美國精神病學專家利博認爲，月球引力能像引起海水潮汐那樣對人體中的液體發生作用，引起人體生物潮。月圓時，易使人感情激動，容易引發胃潰瘍、肺結核出血及心絞痛等疾病。精神病人也會因此更加煩躁不安。

人的情緒變化是一種十分複雜的生理、心理現象，月球的運行變化與人體生理的關係只是影響情緒變化的因素之一。

Source: Newspaper article in the Pacific Weekly, ca. July 1975

So Tung-Po, the great Sung poet, in one of his poems vividly depicts the effects of the evolution of the moon on the mentality and mood of human beings by saying that "people have joys and sorrows/just as the moon is changeable." Modern science has, through the studies of astronomical physics and biological magnetic field, showed that changes of the moon have close relation with the health and the mood of the human body. A US psychiatrist has said that the gravity of the moon will create effects on the fluid within the human body, just as it does with the tides. When the moon is full, people tend to be more emotional, which may easily cause such diseases as gastric ulcer, bleeding of pulmonary tuberculosis, and angina pectoris. People with psychiatric problems may also become more restless…The change in human moods is a very complicated physical and psychological phenomenon. The effect of the evolution of the moon upon the human body is only one of many factors.

一年混沌氣象

FIGURE II.10: *Chinese yeardial*

The Four Seasons in a Year

During the yearlong orbit of the Earth around the sun, Yin and Yang manifest as the four seasons. The twelve cycles of the moon represent one year with four seasons.

The Chinese solar calendar is based on the solar year—the time it takes for Earth to complete one revolution around the sun. The calendar divides the solar year into twenty-four *Chi*, or "breaths." Each breath is just over fifteen days long.

As each breath is a division of the solar year, it follows that each is actually a division of the *ecliptic*, the sun's apparent path through the sky. The twenty-four breaths are paired into twelve "festivals," or solar terms. These "festivals" create twelve divisions of the ecliptic that would be the exact equivalent of the Western zodiacal signs but for one thing—the Chinese propensity to reckon time by the *midpoints* of periods rather than the beginnings. As a consequence, each of the twelve festivals is actually the latter half of one sign, and the beginning half of the next. Most Chinese astrologers reckon the allotted span of life from the lunar and solar calendars. Therefore, as the dates of solar phenomena vary slightly from year to year, the dates for the commencement of each of the twenty-four Chi for each century are carefully calculated.

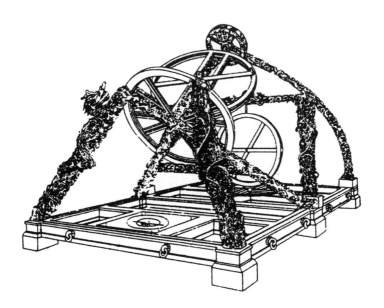

FIGURE II.11: *Chinese astronomers used devices like this one to chart the courses of celestial bodies to measure time.*

Source: Derek Walters, The Chinese Astrology Workbook. *Northamptonshire, England: Aquarian Press, 1988*

TABLE II.4: **The Twenty-Four Chi**

立春	1.	Li Ch'un	Spring commences	Midpoint of Aquarius
雨水	2.	Yü Shui	Rain water	Sun enters Pisces
驚	3.	Ching Chih	Insects waken	Midpoint of Pisces
春分	4.	Ch'un Fen	Spring Equinox	Sun enters Aries
清明	5.	Ch'ing Ming	Clear and Bright	Midpoint of Aries
穀雨	6.	Ku Yü	Corn Rain	Sun enters Taurus
立夏	7.	Li Ch'un	Summer commences	Midpoint of Taurus
小滿	8.	Hsiao Man	Corn sprouting	Sun enters Gemini
芒種	9.	Mang Chung	Corn in ear	Midpoint of Gemini
夏至	10.	Hsia Chih	Summer Solstice	Sun enters Cancer
小暑	11.	Hsiao Shu	Little Heat	Midpoint of Cancer
大暑	12.	Ta Shu	Great Heat	Sun enters Leo
立秋	13.	Li Ch'iu	Autumn commences	Midpoint of Leo
處暑	14.	Ch'u Shu	Heat finishes	Sun enters Virgo
白露	15.	Pai Lu	White Dew	Midpoint of Virgo
秋分	16.	Ch'iu Fen	Autumn Equinox	Sun enters Libra
寒露	17.	Han Lu	Cold Dew	Midpoint of Libra
霜降	18.	Shuang Chiang	Frost descends	Sun enters Scorpio
立冬	19.	Li Tung	Winter commences	Midpoint of Scorpio
小雪	20.	Hsiao Hsüeh	Little Snow	Sun enters Sagittarius
大雪	21.	Ta Hsüeh	Great Snow	Midpoint of Sagittarius
冬至	22.	Tung Chih	Winter Solstice	Sun enters Capricorn
小寒	23.	Hsiao Han	Little cold	Midpoint of Capricorn
大寒	24.	Ta Han	Great cold	Sun enters Aquarius

Spring is a time to work and plant seeds and ideas. Yang energy begins to rise, and days get longer after the spring equinox, during which day and night are exactly the same length.

Summer, with the most light, is the time of growing and getting results. Yang climaxes at the summer solstice, the longest day of the year.

Autumn is a time for harvesting and receiving the fruits of labor. After the autumnal equinox, Yin energy begins to dominate.

Winter is for gathering and storing energy when the light is least available. Yin peaks in the winter solstice, the shortest day of the year.

Tea
（茶）

The tea-plant, which is chiefly grown in Fukien, Chekiang and Kuangtung, is not indigenous to China, and is said to have been imported in C.E. 543 by an ascetic from northern India, and in the ninth century it was in general use as a national beverage. Tea was first introduced into Europe towards the close of the sixteenth century by the Dutch.

The word "tea" is said to be derived from the Fukienese pronunciation ta, and "that excellent, and by all Physitians approved, China Drink, called by the Chineans *Tcha,* by other Nations *Tay* alias Tee," was advertised for sale three centuries ago (in the Weekley Newes, 31 January, 1606) at the Sultaness Head, a coffee house in Sweetings Rents, near the Royal Exchange, London. The Chinese term *ch'a* (茶), "tea" is said to be identical with *k'u t'u* (苦捈), or *t'u* (茶), "chicory," often referred to in the Classics, but during the reign of a prince in the Han dynasty the later name for tea was interdicted, and is now chiefly used to signify "poison." The classical term *ming* (茗) was introduced during the T'ang dynasty, and is still employed in literary composition; it originally denoted the late pickings of the tea-plant. Lu Yü

(陸羽), who died in A.D. 804, was the author of the "Tea Classic" (茶經), a famous work on Tea, and is worshipped by the tea-planters as their tutelary deity.

The time for sowing tea seeds is about the month of September. Holes are dug, each hole being about three feet square, and nine or ten seeds are planted in each hole. When the seedling has grown to the height of a few inches, the planter clears away any grass that may be growing round it.... The best tea generally grows on high mountain peaks, where fogs and snow prevail, which gives a better flavour to the leaves."[1] "The tea-plant yields its first crop at the end of the third year, and thereafter three to four crops are taken annually. The first picking takes place while the leaf is still unfolded."[2]

The tea-shrub of Central China is the *Thea chinensis*, or *Thea viridis* of the botanists, and the leaves are perhaps more lanceolate than those of the *Thea Cantoniensis*, or *Thea assamica*, of the southern regions. "As a result of long cultivation and promiscuous planting, there is hardly a tea garden but is mainly filled with hybrids between these two species."[3] "Both the green and black, or reddish, varieties of the tea-leaf may be produced from either plant. The leaves are picked at three or more occasions in the year, the first picking, which is the best, taking place in April. The leaves are slightly dried in the sun, crushed by the feet of coolies in tubs, in order to get rid of the useless watery juices, and to give a twist to the leaf. The leaf undergoes a series of heatings at a low temperature, is winnowed, picked and packed in lead-lined chests which are arranged in 'chops' of from four hundred to six hunderd and fifty chests."[4]

"The adulturants of tea are extremely numerous, and the Chinese show great skill in this direction. Among adulterants that are used are the leaves of the ash, plum, dog-rose, *Rhamus spp., Rhododendron spp., and Chrysanthemum spp.,* as well as tea stalks and paddy husks. The scented flowers of the *Olea fragrans, Chloranthus inconspicuus, Aglaia odorata, Camelia Susanqua, Gardenia florida, Jasminum Sambac* and other species, are used to give fragrance to inferior qualities. Sometimes the true tea is almost replaced by a factitious compound known as 'lie-tea' which is composed of a little tea dust blended with foriegn leaves, sand and magnetic iron by means of a solution of starch, and coloured with graphite, turmeric, indigo, Prussian blue or China clay, according to the kind of tea it is desired to simulate."[5] The leaves of the *Sageretia theezans* (檟), together with those of the willow, poplar, and spiroea, provide the poor with passable substitutes for tea.

Brick tea (磚茶) is made of tea dust steamed and pressed into hard cakes. The *Camelia oliefera* (山茶) also belongs to the genus *Thea* (order *Ternstroemiacaes*), and yields the so-called tea-oil (茶油), which is expressed from the seeds.

"Tea is described in the Pen Ts'ao (本草), or Herbal, as cooling, peptic, exhilirating, rousing, both laxative and astringent, diuretic, emmenagogue, and, in large concentrated doses, emetic. Taken in large quantities for a long time it is believed to make people thin and anaemic. Weak tea is a favourite wash for bad eyes and sore places. Tea-seeds (茶子) are said to benefit coughs, dyspnoea, and singing in the head."[6]

AUTHORITIES

[1] *Catalogue of the Collection of Chinese Exhibits at the Lousiana Purchase Exposition*, St. Louis, 1904, p. 267.
[2] Dingle and Pratt: *Far Eastern Products Manual*, No. 219.
[3] *Loc. cit.*, No. 219.
[4] Smith: *Contributions towards the Matreia Medica and Natural History of China*: TEA.
[5] Dingle and Pratt: *Far Eastern Products Manual*, No. 219.
[6] Smith: *Contributions towards the Matreia Medica and Natural History of China*: TEA.

Source: C. A. S. Williams, Outline of Chinese Symbolism and Art Motifs. *New York: Dover Publications, Inc., 1976.*

Teas for Each Season of the Year

Farmers refer to the calendar to time their planting and harvests, and the Chinese people use the knowledge embodied in the Chinese calendar to adjust their diet and nutrition to the seasons.

It is good to drink Green tea in the spring.

Summer is the season to drink Dragon Well tea.

Jasmine tea should be drunk during autumn.

Puh Ehr tea with chrysanthemum flower should be drunk in a mild tea during winter.

冬喝普洱加菊花

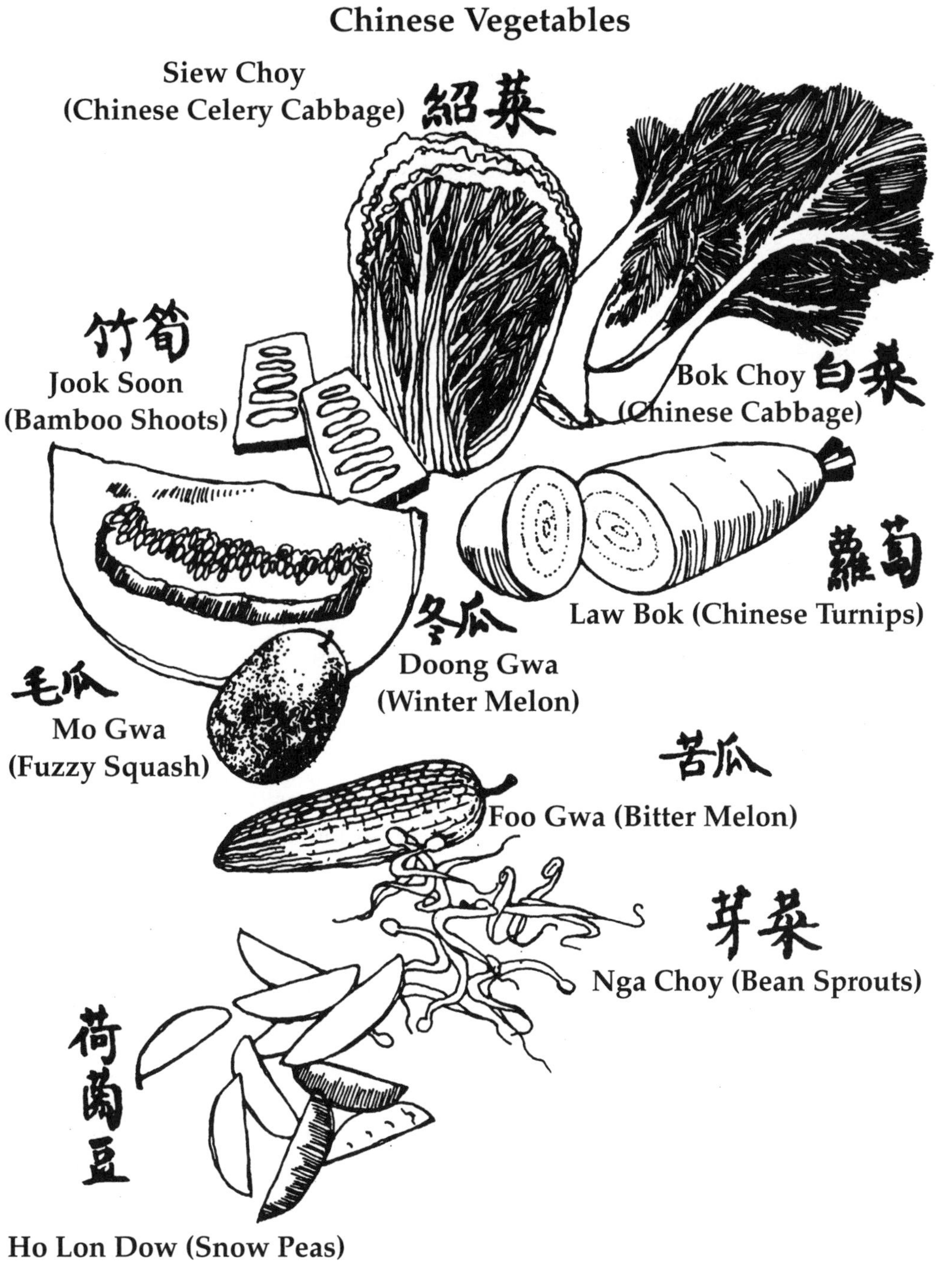

Chinese Vegetables

Siew Choy
(Chinese Celery Cabbage) 紹菜

竹筍
Jook Soon
(Bamboo Shoots)

Bok Choy
(Chinese Cabbage) 白菜

蘿蔔

毛瓜
Mo Gwa
(Fuzzy Squash)

冬瓜
Doong Gwa
(Winter Melon)

Law Bok (Chinese Turnips)

苦瓜
Foo Gwa (Bitter Melon)

芽菜
Nga Choy (Bean Sprouts)

荷蘭豆

Ho Lon Dow (Snow Peas)

FIGURE II.12: *Common Chinese Vegetables*

Source: Shirley Sun, Chinese Food: Teacher's Guide. *San Francisco: Chinese Cultural Foundation, 1976.*

Common Chinese Vegetables

1. Siew Choy 紹菜, or Wong Nga Bok 黃芽白 (Chinese Celery Cabbage) Predominantly long wide white stalks, with crinkly light-green leaves on edges of stalks. Shaped like a head of celery, but chunkier, it is used either for stir-frying or quick soups.

2. Bok Choy 白菜, (Chinese Cabbage) Available all year, an inexpensive staple vegetable. Young stalks of a milk-white color are edged with loose green leaves. The vegetable has a yellow flower in the center.

3. Jook Soon 竹荀, (Bamboo Shoots) 3 to 4 inches long, used often in soups and dishes. Available either fresh, or, more commonly, in cans.

4. Law Bok 蘿蔔, (Chinese Turnips) Plentiful and best in winter, this long white turnip is used for long-simmer soups, smother-cook dishes, and stir-frying.

5. Doong Gwa 冬瓜, (Winter Melon) In actuality a squash, in season during the wintertime, hence, the name. Very large, with a green skin, and a chalky white dust which scrapes off. The flesh is of ivory color, and used in soups.

6. Mo Gwa 毛瓜, (Fuzzy Squash) Apple green in color, with tiny white hairs. Popular in soups and stir-fry dishes. About 4 inches long.

7. Foo Gwa 苦瓜, (Bitter Melon) This is really a member of the squash family, and grows on a vine. It has a linear, pebbly surface, smooth and jade-like in texture and color. When split open, the inside pulpy sponge and red seeds must be removed before cooking. It has a cool, slightly bitter flavor, and is used with meats and fish.

8. Nga Choy 芽菜, (Bean Sprouts) Bean sprouts are tiny shoots which grow from either a mung bean or soy bean. Mung bean sprouts are smaller, about 1 inch long, while soy bean sprouts may be from 2 to 3 inches long. They are used in various dishes.

9. Ho Lon Dow 荷蘭豆, (Snow Peas) These are also called Sugar Peas. They are 3 to 4 inches long, and about 1 inch wide. Break off tips and de-string them before cooking. They are sold cheapest from May through September.

Source: Adapted from Johnny Kan, Eight Immortal Flavors. *pp. 83–87.*

The Chinese Zodiac

FIGURE II.13: *Twelve Animals of the Chinese Zodiac*

The chart in FIGURE II.13 gives an introduction to the characteristics of the twelve animals of the Chinese Zodiac. Each animal represents a year in the twelve-year cycle of the Chinese calendar, and each animal has specific talents, which can be enhanced with training. These short descriptions provide an opportunity for self-understanding of personal Yang and Yin character traits. For example, the horse is said to be attractive yet impatient, the dog is loyal yet stubborn, the snake wise yet vain. Your animal's characteristics may explain to you your tendencies in personal behavior and your compatibility with other signs. Reading more about your own character can aid you in improving your life by seeing deeper into your own nature. One can examine and emphasize certain traits while revising and diminishing others.

The Chinese Zodiac
中國十二生肖年屬表

1942, 1954, 1966, 1978, 1990, 2002
Popular and attractive to the opposite sex. You are often ostentatious and impatient. You need people. Marry a Tiger or a Dog early, but never a Rat. Horse

1943, 1955, 1967, 1979, 1991, 2003
Elegant and creative, you are timid and prefer anonymity. You are most compatible with Boars and Rabbits but never the Ox. Sheep

1944, 1956, 1968, 1980, 1992, 2004
You are very intelligent and are able to influence people. An enthusiastic achiever, you are easily discouraged and confused. Avoid Tigers. Seek a Dragon or a Rat. Monkey

1945, 1957, 1969, 1981, 1993, 2005
A pioneer in spirit, you are devoted to work and quest after knowledge. You are selfish and eccentric. Rabbits are trouble. Snakes and Oxen are fine. Rooster

1946, 1958, 1970, 1982, 1994, 2006
Loyal and honest you work well with others. Generous yet stubborn and often selfish. Look to the Horse or Tiger. Watch out for Dragons. Dog

1947, 1959, 1971, 1983, 1995, 2007
Noble and chivalrous. Your friends will be lifelong, yet you are prone to marital strife. Avoid other Boars. Marry a Rabbit or a Sheep. Boar

1936, 1948, 1960, 1972, 1984, 1996
You are very ambitious yet honest. Prone to spend freely. Seldom make lasting friendships. Most compatible with Dragons and Monkeys Least compatible with Horses. Rat

1937, 1949, 1961, 1973, 1985, 1997
Bright, patient and inspiring to others. You can be happy by yourself. yet make an outstanding parent. Marry a Snake or Cock. The Sheep will bring trouble. Ox

1938, 1950, 1962, 1974, 1986, 1998
Tiger people are aggressive, courageous, candid and sensitive. Look to the horse and Dog for happiness. Beware of the Monkey. Tiger

1939, 1951, 1963, 1975, 1987, 1999
Luckiest of all signs, you are also talented and articulate. Affectionate, yet shy, you seek peace throughout your life. Marry a Sheep or Boar. Your opposite is the Cock. Rabbit

1940, 1952, 1964, 1976, 1988, 2000
You are eccentric and your life complex. You have a very passionate nature and abundant health. Marry a Monkey or Rat late in life. Avoid the Dog.  Dragon

1941, 1953, 1965, 1977, 1989, 2001
Wise and intense with a tendency towards physical beauty. Vain and high tempered. The Boar is your enemy. The Cock or Ox are your best signs. Snake

FIGURE II.14: *Animals of the Chinese zodiac*

Palmistry

Ancient Chinese fortunetellers used their palms to tell the twelve zodiac characters and their meaning in the twenty-four hours of the day to predict fortunes and personal characteristics.

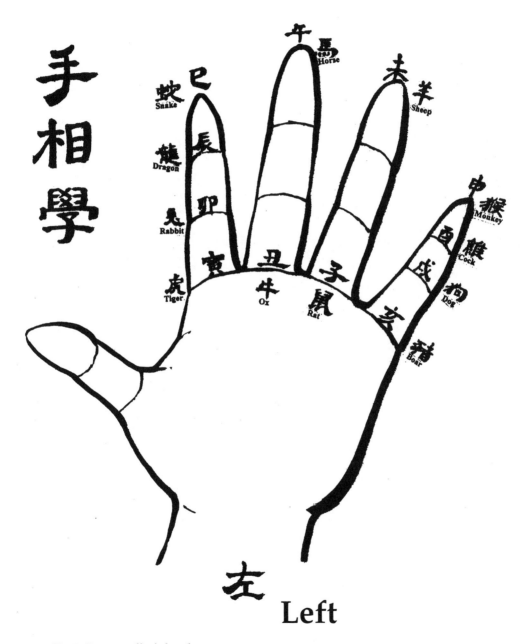

FIGURE II.15: *Fortuneteller's hand map*

The *I Ching*

The *I Ching*, or *Book of Changes*, represents the first comprehensive canonization of Tai-Chi philosophy, and is considered the most ancient book of wisdom in China. It provides a kind of "unified theory" of the way in which the creative process of the Tao unfolds. This book has been used over time to help explain such things as the creation of the universe, the evolution of life, the formation and development of the human body, the arising of ideas, and ever-subtler experiences of the process of change. The *I Ching* describes patterns of this dynamic creative process and outlines a way for humans to align themselves with the changing cycles of nature so that they may live in harmony with the world around them.

FIGURE II.16: *Simmone Kuo at Fu Hsi's Temple*

The *I Ching* describes the process of change using Fu Hsi's symbols of broken and solid lines to represent Yin and Yang. Once Yin and Yang poles are recognized within Tai-Chi, one can distinguish various stages of change between them. The next level of detail is represented in the *I Ching* by adding another solid or broken line to the foundation Yin or Yang lines to form four digrams (FIGURE II.17).

| OLD YANG | YOUNG YIN | OLD YIN | YOUNG YANG |

FIGURE II.17: *The digrams*

The "old" digrams are considered stable, and the "young" digrams are understood to be stages of change between the stable modes. As Yin and Yang define the extremes, the digrams represent levels of change between them. As Yin and Yang represent day and night, the digrams describe dawn, noon, dusk, and midnight. As Yin and Yang peak on the winter and summer solstices, the digrams define the seasons of spring, summer, fall, and winter. They help to describe the transformations between Yin and Yang with more detail.

As evolution continues, these forces interact, creating new polarities among themselves, and complexity again increases. By adding another solid or broken line to the top of each digram to describe these new possibilities, we reveal the eight trigrams, representing nature's elemental energies: Heaven, Wind, Water, Mountain, Earth, Thunder, Fire, and Lake (FIGURE II.18).

Heaven (Creative)   **Wind (Gentle)**   **Water (Mystery)**   **Mountain (Stubborn)**

Earth (Receptive)   **Thunder (Arousing)**   **Fire (Clarity)**   **Lake (Open)**

FIGURE II.18: *The eight trigrams*

Just as the digrams gave more detail to the stages between Yin and Yang poles, trigrams allow us another level of definition with which to explain our world. The trigrams are also symbolic of seasons, colors, body parts, personality traits, and directions. The Eight Trigrams are thus images of the movement from Yin to Yang and from Yang to Yin. As Yin and Yang distinguish man and woman, the trigrams describe a family. They describe life stages between the poles of life and death and bring color to Yin and Yang's black and white. We can recognize their appearance in the world around us in the phenomena of TABLE II.5.

TABLE II.5: **Trigram Energies and Characteristics**

Heaven	Lake	Fire	Thunder	Wind	Water	Mountain	Earth
☰	☱	☲	☳	☴	☵	☶	☷
Ch'ien	**Tui**	**Li**	**Chen**	**Sun**	**K'an**	**Ken**	**K'un**
乾	兌	離	震	巽	坎	艮	坤
Northwest	West	South	East	Southeast	North	Northeast	Southwest
Firm	Joyous	Clinging	Arousing	Gentle	Abyss	Keeping Still	Yielding
Head	Mouth	Eye	Foot	Thigh	Heart	Hand	Belly
Death	Adolescent	Conception	Birth	Childhood	Embryo	Maturity	Before Birth

The Relationship between the Eight Trigrams and the Kinship of Human Beings
(In Chinese)

八卦配屬人物

八卦等於天、地、風、雷、水、火、山、澤沼。八卦除配天、地、風、雷、水、火、山、澤之外，復配有五行。計：乾爲金，坤爲土，震爲木，艮爲土，離爲火，坎爲木，兌爲金，巽爲木。根據上面的五行分配，就很容易分出東四宅與西四宅了。首先明白，乾兌兩卦同是金，艮坤兩卦同是土，震巽兩卦同是木，離卦屬火，坎卦屬水。五行有相生相剋，土是生金，因此土與金同在一起是相生，乾兌與艮坤就成爲西四宅了，因爲兌卦在正西方，乾卦在西北方也。五行是水生木、土生火，因此震巽離坎一起，就成爲東方位，巽卦在東南方。緊記上述的五行生剋，很容易知道自己是東四命人，抑或是西四命人。

八卦的天地、風雷、山澤、水火，每一對都是相生相成，亦可以說，天地間的萬事萬物，全是由八卦構成。古籍所載的：「天地水火合宜而植物生，有本有用故動物作，天地氤氳、乾坤交媾而萬化生，以金爲器具而文明成焉。」人事日繁文明愈演進，聖人仰觀俯察，將八卦演進爲八八六十四卦，最後作六十四卦爲易經。中國的術數，絕大部份是以易經爲藍本，指導人們趨吉避兇，但由於易經文字艱澀，很多人不容易理解。八卦圖有「先天八卦」，亦有「後天八卦」由於兩個圖都十分復雜，很難用簡單文字說明，而一般讀者亦未必有興趣！現在將八卦與人物六親的關係，分述於後，乾爲父，坤爲母，震爲長男、巽爲長女、坎爲中男、離爲中女、艮爲少男、兌爲少女。

The Relationship between the Eight Trigrams and the Kinship of Human Beings

Ch'ien		Father
K'un		Mother
Chen		Oldest son
Sun		Oldest daughter
K'an		Second son
Li		Second daughter
Ken		Youngest son
Tui		Youngest daughter

乾爲父，坤爲母，震爲長男、巽爲長女、坎爲中男、離爲中女、艮爲少男、兌爲少女。

現在將八卦與人物六親的關係，分述於後，

FIGURE II.19: *Chinese family hierarchy*

FIGURE II.20: *Tai-Chi with Pa Kua (eight trigrams)*

The trigrams are archetypes for increasingly complex forms of energy. As the trigrams interact in different ways, the various elemental energies combine to give form to the sixty-four hexagrams, the level of manifestation on which the *I Ching* is based. By combining any two of these trigrams, one on top of another, to form a hexagram, sixty-four combinations are possible. These are understood as a set of archetypal situations whose transformations both shape and describe the cosmos.

The hexagrams represent all the possible states of change in the universe. Together they describe, in even finer detail than the digrams or trigrams, a complete cycle of evolution, from Yin to Yang and back to Yin, from creation through myriad transformative changes to destruction. Every individual thing—from an atom to a mountain, a body part or entire person, community, or planet—can be seen as a Tai-Chi, with its own Yin and Yang aspects, moving through the continuously changing transitional energies represented by the hexagrams. The digrams, trigrams, and hexagrams give increasing detail of movement between stages and poles.

Eight Diagrams

The Pa Kua, or Eight Diagrams, are represented by an arrangement of certain cabalistic signs consisting of various combinations of straight lines arranged in a circle, said to have been evolved from the markings on the shell of a tortoise by the legendary Emperor Fu Hsi, 2852 B.C.E. They are also said to have been created from the two primary forms, represented by a continuous straight line called Yang I, or the symbol of the male principle, and a broken line called Yin I, or the symbol of the female principle (vide Yin and Yang). Mathematics are said to have been derived from the Eight Diagrams, which figuratively denote the evolution of nature and its cyclic changes.

Wen Wang, 1231–1135 B.C.E., the founder of the Chou dynasty, while undergoing imprisonment at the hands of the tyrant Emperor Chou Hsin, devoted himself to a study of the Diagrams (and the series of 64 hexagrams constructed by taking these two at a time), and appended to each of them certain explanations entitled "the Judgement", which, with further observations termed "the Lines", attributed to his son Chon Kung, constitute the abstruse work known as the "Canon of Changes", the most venerated and least understood of the Chinese classics, serving as a basis for the philosophy of divination and geomancy, and supposed to contain the elements of metaphysical knowledge and the clue to the secrets of creation…

A plaque made of copper, silver, or jade, and engraved with the Eight Diagrams, is considered to have the power of preserving the wearer from misfortune, and assuring his future prosperity. It may also be nailed over a house door as an emblem of felicity.

Source: C. A. S. Williams, Outline of Chinese Symbolism and Art Motifs. *New York: Dover Publications, Inc., 1976.*

Introduction to King Wen and the Duke of Chou

(In Chinese)

周易概說

上古時期，隨着生產活动的发展，人们开始现自世界的一些规律，尤其是在事物发展生長展中起决定作用的两种对立因素，以为这两种立相消长缺一不可的因素是任何事物都具有并且固有的属性。後来人们将其中一方称"陰"另一方称"陽"，開始形成中國文化特有的"陰""陽"思念。

King Wen and the Duke of Chou

King Chou Wen-Wang (1231–1135 B.C.E.) and his son, the Duke of Chou, are credited with writing explanations and images for each of the hexagrams, and explanations of the moving lines, respectively. Chou Wen-Wang, progenitor of the Chou Dynasty, was imprisoned at the age of eighty-two for seven years during a time of upheaval between dynasties. Wen devoted the time of his imprisonment to the study of philosophy and the *I Ching*, and reflected on his life and the nature of the world. He observed the cyclical change of creation and destruction in all phenomena: from the seasonal shifts of the solar year to the movement of the celestial bodies; from the rise and fall of dynasties, to the life span of an individual.

Wen was particularly fascinated by the precision with which various phenomena present themselves in nature: the teeming of insects after the ground has cracked open at the end of winter, the massing of swallows for migration after the autumn's first cold dew, the predictability of tides, and the waxing and waning of the moon. Through his meditation on the system of trigrams and hexagrams of Fu Hsi, Wen was enlightened with a deep understanding of the workings of nature. From this perspective, he developed the sequence of sixty-four hexagrams, which, after three millennia, is still in use today in the traditional *I Ching*. He created the first comprehensive commentaries on the *I Ching*, including the "judgment" for each hexagram, together with line-by-line commentaries for each of its six lines. Wen's son, Duke Chou Jung, the founder of the Chou Dynasty, later combined and collated Wen's interpretation of each of the sixty-four hexagrams with his own interpretations of the moving lines, to provide the oldest existing written version of the *I Ching*.

FIGURE II.21: *The sixty-four hexagrams*

The hexagrams appear in a natural sequence in the *Book of Changes*, along with commentary and images to give the reader a deeper understanding of the universal principle of each representative symbol. Each hexagram is capable of changing into any other through the polar reversal of any or all of its Yin or Yang lines. The *I Ching* explains how the sixty-four hexagrams move and transform into each other within this natural cycle. The *Book* records the evolution of complexity from the fundamental polarities of Yin and Yang through the archetypal energies of the sixty-four hexagrams, as they move from emptiness through the phenomenal forms of Being back to emptiness again.

Confucius

Confucius, the great philosopher and educator of China, was born in 551 B.C.E. in Qufu, Shandong Province. He lived during the Spring and Autumn Periods of the Zhou Dynasty, a time when there were many philosophers. During the Zhou Dynasty, there was complete disorder, and the emperor faced poverty. The focus of the government was switched from Heaven to the people, and government policy was enriched, developed, and systematized. This provided an environment for learning in which the political atmosphere was initially conducive to the development of a new ideology. After much study, research, and travel, Confucius created a school in Qufu in which, as in Plato's academy, students inquired into the whole of life. Ethics and human relationships were the central concerns of Confucius's teaching, while patience, tolerance, and correctness were the virtues he cherished.

Confucius analyzed and annotated the *I Ching* six centuries (approximately sixth century B.C.E.) after King Wen and his son, the Duke of Chou, compiled the *Book of Changes*. He wrote commentaries to the judgments and images of King Wen. He said of the *Book of Changes*, "If I had more years to my life I would devote them to the study of the *I Ching*."

Contexts of the *I Ching*

The *I Ching* is a key to the great treasure house of the mind, for humanity and the human mind arise from nature and the principles it embodies. In the hands of one who understands its potential, the *I Ching* becomes a tool for directed inquiry and contemplation of any aspect of the cosmos: the cycles of natural phenomena, the structure of human society, the genetic code, the process of natural selection, the formation and development of a human body, the binary language of computer programming, the changing of the seasons, the principles of individual psychology, as well as the world of ideas and more. The patterns in the *I Ching* show us how the Tao gives form to chaos—a continual process that we can observe in the world around us. The *I Ching* can be read many ways: as a divination tool, a description of the creation of the universe, a textbook of the movements of Tai-Chi Chuan, or a manual describing the course of psychic energy (Chi) in meditation, for just a few examples.

In addition to its uses as a key to understanding, the *I Ching* has been consulted as a wise oracle in China for thousands of years, showing questioners where they stand within the cycle of changes in regard to specific situations about which they ask. By throwing yarrow stalks assigned specific numbers, certain hexagrams appear to the questioner, relating to their present circumstances. "Changing lines" in the hexagrams (denoted by their numerical value) show when a certain line within the hexagram is climaxing and about to experience a polar reversal that will change the hexagram into a new one and take it beyond the original sequence. The cycle of change in the *I Ching* is not a fixed, deterministic chain reaction that unfolds in the same way each time, but an evolving process capable of random, spontaneous changes leading to novel situations. This process, like recent experiments in quantum mechanics, is changed by the consciousness of the observer, in this case the questioner. By being aware of his or her current position, the questioner can more fully understand the situation, and align him or herself with the energies of nature to live in greater harmony with the world around them.

The *I Ching* is also the first known application of binary mathematics. During the seventeenth century, one of the Jesuit missionaries in China, Father Joachim Bouvet, returned to Europe, and showed the Table of Hexagrams from the *I Ching* to Gottfried Wilhelm Leibniz (1646–1716), a well-known German philosopher and mathematician (father of modern calculus). Leibniz was amazed and moved by the unbelievable similarity of the binary mathematics system he had been working on and the hexagram table of the *I Ching* from approximately 2865 B.C.E. The *I Ching*'s pattern of 1, 2, 4, 8, 16, 32, 64, (Tai-Chi, Yin and Yang, digrams, trigrams, on to hexagrams) is in binary scale; they are equal to 2^0, 2^1, 2^2, 2^3, 2^4, 2^5, 2^6. This connection led Leibniz to the discovery of a functioning binary system. Leibniz was astonished to discover that if one substitutes "1" for each broken line and "0" for each solid line, and then proceeds through the sixty-four hexagrams in order, one finds the sequence 000000, 000001, 000010, 000011, and so forth. This is the binary notation for the decimal numbers 0 through 63. This is the same mathematical system that all computer languages are based on today. As Martin Gardner said, "It was not until the time of Leibniz that the Fu Hsi sequence was recognized as being isomorphic with a useful arithmetical notation" ("Mathematical Games," *Scientific American*, January 1974).

The hexagram system is a dual-value system, with Yin and Yang acting like ON and OFF circuitry, 1 and 0 in computer programming language. The Yin (— —) represents the open circuit, or 1, the OFF position, because the middle of the broken line is open. The Yang (—) is associated with the closed circuit, or 0, the ON position, because the center of the solid line is closed. The human nervous system also works on a binary system, as does genetics and natural selection.

III

Yin-Yang in Tai-Chi Chuan

FIGURE III.1: *Simmone Kuo teaches Tai-Chi philosophy in the Advanced Tai-Chi Chuan class at San Francisco State University.*

Yin-Yang in Tai-Chi Chuan

Through contemplation and careful application of the principles of the *I Ching,* the Tai-Chi Chuan form was created on Wu Tang Mountain as a way to harmonize with these universal principles. Chan San Feng and an anonymous Taoist friend derived movements from Shao-lin Chuan, Pa Kua, and Shing Yi, and based the Tai-Chi Chuan form on the tenets of Taoist philosophy. The name of this internal martial art form, "Fist of Balance," relates to the harmonious balancing of Yin and Yang energies in the body through movement and awareness. The complementarity and transmutability of the two opposing forces, Yin and Yang, are exhibited in the circular and changing Tai-Chi Chuan movements. Feet, knees, legs, waist, hands, and head move in harmonious sequence, changing from Yin to Yang as weight shifts, legs kick, the body turns, and arms perform their movements.

Just as the *I Ching* consists of a sequence of sixty-four hexagrams, the traditional form of Tai-Chi Chuan consists of a sequence of sixty-four movements. This system was originally a closely guarded secret that was passed on from the Master to selected students.

The human body, like all things, arises from the Tao, is composed of Yin and Yang aspects, and goes through changes as described by the hexagrams in the *I Ching.* The principles of the *Book of Changes* exist within us just as they do in the rest of nature; thus the body as a whole can be seen to represent the entire universe in microcosm. The top half of the body, above the navel, is considered Yang, compared to the lower half, below the navel, which is understood to be Yin; the front is Yin while the back is Yang; the left side of the body is seen as Yang and the right as Yin. All polarities are balanced in the body's center, known as the *tan-tien.* The tan-tien is located approximately 3 inches below the navel, mid-distance between the front of the body and the lumbar area of the spine known as the *ming men* or "gate of life." It is the body's center of gravity as well as the "sea of Chi." It is here that the Chi is gathered in Tai-Chi Chuan and where the body's movements originate.

The exterior of the body is considered Yang and the interior Yin, with all the internal organs given their own Yin and Yang associations (see "Chinese Medicine" in section II). By moving the body, with all its universally symbolic parts, through postures that align specific meridians and energy centers, turning through the four directions, while maintaining the interchange of Yin and Yang through natural breathing, the Tai-Chi student aligns his or her body/mind with universal energies and becomes an individual part in harmony with the larger, unfolding pattern around them.

TABLE III.1: **Five Steps of Tai-Chi Chuan Related to the Five Elements and Five Directions**

Earth	On guard	Center
Wood	Retreat	East
Metal	Advance	West
Fire	Shift right	South
Water	Shift left	North

As the feet move through the steps of TABLE III.1, one leg remains "full" or compressed, supporting the body's weight, and representing the Yang principle, while the other is "empty" and relaxed, being the Yin aspect. The legs continuously reverse polarities; the "empty" leg is filled and the "full" leg is emptied as balance shifts and the movement progresses. The five steps of Tai-Chi Chuan move the student through the five elemental phases of Taoist philosophy and incorporate the five directions (TABLE III.1), while the eight hand postures express the trigrams (TABLE III.2)

TABLE III.2: **Eight Hands of Tai-Chi Chuan**

Heaven	Ward off	Northwest
Earth	Roll back	Southwest
Water	Press	North
Fire	Push	South
Wind	Pull	Southeast
Thunder	Split	East
Lake	Elbow	West
Mountain	Shoulder	Northeast

Each of the sixty-four Tai-Chi movements is related to a hexagram of the *I Ching*. As the lower body moves through the five elemental phases and the middle body follows the changes of the trigrams, the head turns to face the four directions, coordinating and unifying the body's three sections, forming fluidly interchanging hexagrams. In the *I Ching*, each hexagram develops out of the previous one, just as each Tai-Chi movement flows smoothly and naturally from the one before it.

Tai-Chi Chuan was developed to facilitate the flow of chi along its twelve major pathways. The practice of the Tai-Chi Chuan form releases energy blocks—physical, mental, and emotional—by facilitating the smooth flowing of healing Chi through the meridians. By balancing the polarities of the body/mind and keeping the organs nourished and healthy, Tai-Chi allows practitioners to extend and brighten their lives.

The Tai-Chi Chuan Form

TABLE III.3: Names of the Sixty-Four Movements (in Chinese)

一	擎掌問佛		三十三	斜單鞭	
二	攬雀尾		三十四	野馬分鬃	6步75度
三	單鞭		三十五	斜單鞭	
四	白鶴掠翅		三十六	雲裡穿梭	
五	摟膝拗步		三十七	轉身攬雀尾	
六	卻步搬攔捶		三十八	單鞭	
七	上步如封似閉		三十九	雲手	2步
八	抱虎歸山	9步	四十	單鞭下勢	
九	肘底錘		四十一	金雞獨立	完於第6步，左腳腳趾向上
十	倒攆猴	8步	四十二	倒攆猴	10步
十一	挫掌斜飛		四十三	挫掌斜飛	
十二	左右提手		四十四	左右提手	
十三	飛履上勢		四十五	飛履上勢	
十四	扇通臂		四十六	扇通臂	
十五	青龍出水		四十七	雙風貫耳	
十六	單鞭		四十八	通天炮	
十七	雲手	6步	四十九	單鞭	
十八	單鞭		五十	雲手	4步
十九	高探馬		五十一	單鞭	
二十	左右分腳		五十二	高探馬	
二十一	轉身蹬腳	向左邊轉身75度	五十三	十字擺蓮	
二十二	風擺荷葉	4步75度	五十四	栽捶	
二十三	指擋捶		五十五	上步攬雀尾	
二十四	翻身二起腳		五十六	單鞭	
二十五	上步搬攔捶		五十七	雲手	4步
二十六	退步臂身		五十八	單鞭下勢	
二十七	迎面踢腳		五十九	上步七星	
二十八	轉身蹬腳	向右邊轉身180度	六十	退步跨虎	
二十九	進步搬攔捶		六十一	斜身扭月	
三十	如封似閉		六十二	擺蓮腳	
三十一	抱虎歸山		六十三	彎弓射虎	
三十二	撇身捶		六十四	左右攬雀尾　　合太極	

TABLE III.4: **Names of the Sixty-Four Movements (in English)**

1. Strike palm to ask Buddha	33. Diagonal single whip
2. Grasp bird's tail	34. Partition of wild horse's mane (6 steps 75degrees)
3. Single whip	35. Diagonal single whip
4. Stork spreads wings	36. Working at shuttles inside clouds
5. Brush knee and twist step	37. Step up and grasp bird's tail
6. Deflect downward, parry and punch	38. Single whip
7. Step up and push with palms	39. Wave hands like clouds (2 steps)
8. Carry tiger to mountain (9 steps)	40. Single whip lowering down
9. Fist under elbow	41. Golden cock stands on one leg
10. Step back and repulse monkey (8 steps)	(finish at the 6th step, left toe up)
11. Slow palm slanting, flying	42. Step back and repulse monkey (10 steps)
12. Raise right (left) hand	43. Slow palm slanting, flying
13. Fly pulling back and step up	44. Raise left (right) hand
14. Fan through the arm	45. Fly pulling back and step up
15. Green dragon dropping water	46. Fan through the arm
16. Single whip	47. Strike opponents ears with both fists
17. Wave hands like clouds (6 steps)	48. Through sky cannon
18. Single whip	49. Single whip
19. High pat on horse	50. Wave hands like clouds (4 steps)
20. Separation of right (left) foot	51. Single whip
21. Turn and kick with sole (turn left 75 degrees)	52. High pat on horse
22. Wind blowing lotus leaf (4 steps 75 degrees)	53. Cross wave of water lily
23. Finger block up with downward fist	54. Downward fist
24. Turn around and kick two feet upward	55. Step up and grasp bird's tail
25. Step up, deflect downward, parry and punch	56. Single whip
26. Step back with arms beside body	57. Wave hands like clouds (4 steps)
27. Left foot kicks up, forward	58. Single whip lowering down
28. Turn and kick with sole (turn right 270 degrees)	59. Step up to form seven stars
	60. Retreat to ride tiger
29. Step forward, deflect downward, parry and punch	61. Slanting body and turn the moon
	62. Wave lotus foot
30. Pull back with palm and push	63. Shoot tiger with bow and arrow
31. Carry tiger to mountain	64. (Right) left grasp bird's tail
32. Chop opponent with fist	- conclusion of grand terminus

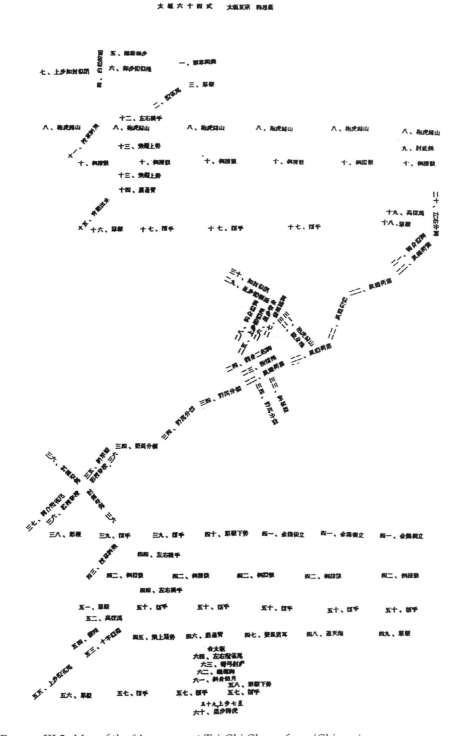

FIGURE III.2: *Map of the 64-movement Tai-Chi Chuan form (Chinese)*

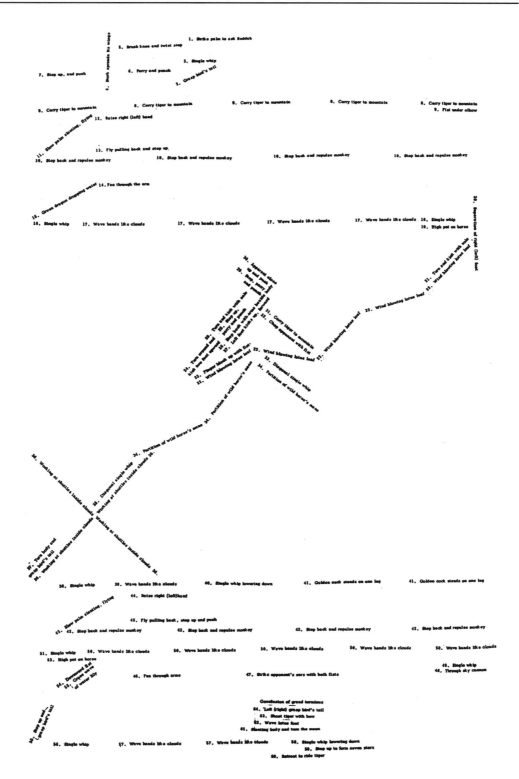

FIGURE III.3: *Map of the 64-movement Tai-Chi Chuan form (English)*

FIGURES III.2 and III.3 show a map of the sixty-four movements that give the Tai-Chi Chuan form its specific shape. It was created to preserve the accuracy of the form. Practitioners of Tai-Chi Chuan should follow it very closely.

Correct Foot Placement for Balance

揽雀尾
GRASP BIRD'S TAIL #2

單鞭
SINGLE WHIP #3, 16, 18, 38, 49, 51, 56

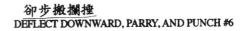

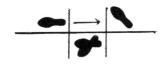

摟膝拗步
BRUSH KNEE AND TWIST STEP #5

卸步搬攔捶
DEFLECT DOWNWARD, PARRY, AND PUNCH #6

倒攆猴
STEP BACK AND REPULSE MONKEY #10, 42

雲手
WAVE HANDS LIKE CLOUDS #17, 39, 50, 57

風擺荷葉
WIND BLOWING LOTUS LEAF #22

Correct Foot Placement for Balance

抱虎歸山
CARRY TIGER TO MOUNTAIN #31

撇身捶
CHOP OPPONENT WITH FIST #32

斜單鞭
DIAGONAL SINGLE WHIP #33, 35

野馬分鬃
PARTITION WILD HORSES MANE #34

雙風貫耳　　　　通天炮
STRIKE OPPONENTS EARS WITH BOTH FISTS #47 to THROUGH SKY CANNON #48

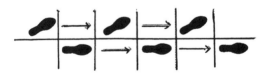

十字擺蓮
CROSS WAVE OF WATER LILY (AFTER KICK) #53

擺蓮脚
WAVE LOTUS FOOT (AFTER KICK) #62

Movement 1: Strike Palm to Ask Buddha

擊手問佛

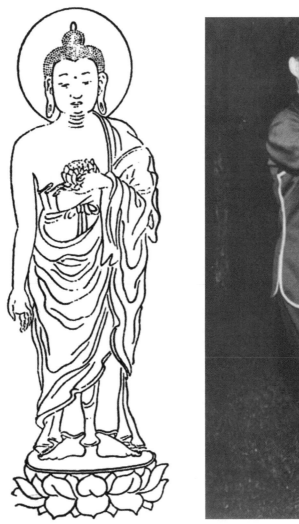 

FIGURE III.4: *One begins Tai-Chi Chuan with a salutation to the Buddha, to encourage mindfulness and nonviolence.*

FIGURE III.5: *Simmone Kuo performs Movement 1: Strike Palm to Ask Buddha.*

Movement 41: Golden Cock Stands on One Leg

金鷄獨立

FIGURE III.13: *In Chinese, the flamingo is called a golden cock because it has a gold tinge to its feathers.*

FIGURE III.14: *The bamboo-like form of the flamingo's legs and the way they walk is visible in Simmone Kuo's performance of Movement 41, Golden Cock Stands on One Leg.*

Movements 17, 39, 50, 57: Wave Hands Like Clouds

雲手

FIGURE III.8: *Sifu Kuo Lien-Ying performs Wave Hands Like Clouds, which is repeated in Movements 17, 39, 50, and 57.*

Movement 15: Green Dragon Dropping Water
青龍出水

FIGURE III.6: *Dragons live in the sea. When they come out, they have to drop the water to reduce their weight so they can fly.*

FIGURE III.7: *Sifu Kuo Lien-Ying imitates the dragon's movements in Movement 15, Green Dragon Dropping Water, by reaching out with both hands, then bringing both hands back, stepping forward, and pushing.*

Movement 22: Wind Blowing Lotus Leaf

:風擺荷葉右勢

FIGURE III.11: *Lotus flowers rise from the mud, but they are not contaminated by it. The lotus flower represents purity, harmony, and courage.*

FIGURE III.12: *Sifu Kuo Lien-Ying performs Movement 22, Wind Blowing Lotus Leaf, which is named after the beautiful lotus flower; it may grow out of mud, yet it never touches the mud. In the autumn when the wind blows, the lotus leaf floats in a zigzag pattern across the water. This Tai-Chi Chuan step zigzags just as the precious flower floats.*

Movement 19 and 52: High Pat on a Horse
高探馬

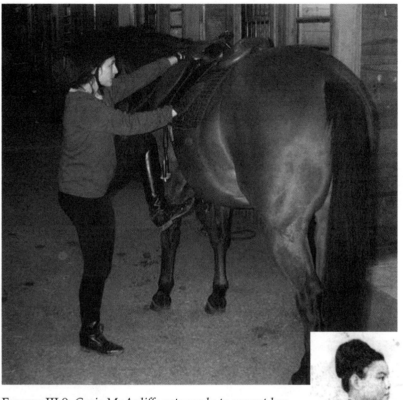

FIGURE III.9: *Carie McAuliffe gets ready to mount her horse, Scooter, in Massachusetts.*

FIGURE III.10: *Simmone Kuo performs Movement 19 (and 52), High Pat on a Horse, which is based on the starting position for climbing onto a horse.*

The Universal Stance

宇宙樁(右式)

FIGURE III.15: *The Universal Stance or "Post of Life"*

The Universal Stance

The Universal Stance or "Post of Life" is an exercise that increases mental concentration, gathers Chi, calms the mind, and harmonizes body/mind energies. This exercise requires that one stand upright and still, not leaning to one side or another. The body's weight is supported by one leg, without that leg being bent or its muscles tightened. The other leg extends forward to serve as a point of balance. The arms are raised forward and spread to form a ring at shoulder height, as if embracing someone. If the right foot is forward, the right hand is outstretched a little farther than the left; if the left foot is forward, the left hand is more outstretched. Breathing is free and natural; eyes gaze straight forward to the horizon. All the muscles in the body are relaxed, allowing blood to flow unconstricted, and the Chi sinks to the tan-tien. Concentration stays on the form.

While in the expression of the Tai-Chi Chuan form, "the inside moves outside," during standing meditation, "the outside moves inside." Whereas Tai-Chi Chuan uses a still mind and active body to move energy through the body's meridians, Tai-Chi meditators use a still body and active mind to circulate chi. This is the classic method used to refine and circulate the body's internal energy (Chi).

Every human being is surrounded by an electromagnetic energy field, with the positive pole in our head and the negative pole in our sacrum. Heavenly (Yang) energy enters the human system at the crown of the head, while Earthly (Yin) energy enters at the base of the spine. These energies enter and are then combined and circulated in the human system through the meridians.

The Universal Stance is a perfect balance for the active Tai-Chi Chuan movements and allows a deeper understanding of the movement of chi within the body. Both practices are manifestations of the creative principles of the universe and allow us to experience these principles within ourselves.

IV

Yin-Yang in Daily Life

Daily Practice

FIGURE IV.1: *Sifu's hand greeting implies, "Thank you for being a good student." In the old days, each dynasty had its own greeting in order to show respect among different Chinese martial arts. At the end of the Ching Dynasty and the establishment of the Republic of China, the deep bending and bowing style was replaced by this simple and elegant hand gesture.*

FIGURE IV.2: *Simu and student Renée Wong meet and exchange Tai-Chi Chuan hand greeting.*

> When practicing Tai-Chi Chuan, the mind must remain quiet
> but alert, with attention concentrated on the movements and the
> positions. The movements should be done as an integrated whole,
> and not as isolated steps. In addition, no movement should be
> forced or strained.
> —SIFU KUO LIEN-YING, *TAI-CHI CHUAN IN THEORY AND PRACTICE*

Good health must be earned with discipline, diligent practice, and hard work.
Master Kuo Lien Ying always said, "Practice every day. Skip one day, lose ten."
The most ideal location for daily practice is outdoors in the open air.

Tai-Chi Chuan is a spiritual practice as well as a mental-physical discipline—a
discipline that can show the student how the spiritual, the mental, and the physical are
one while at the same time separate. While practicing, "the whole concentration of the
mind is … on the spirit …" (Sifu). Tai-Chi Chuan is a holistic system of movement that
encourages the harmonious development of the entire human being, by integrating
mind and body and bringing the body's polarities to a state of wholeness.

The correct practice of Tai-Chi Chuan relies on thought and mental concentration as well as muscular strength and flexibility. If thought, as opposed to strength, propels each movement, then the Chi will flow through the body unobstructed by tension. It is this flowing energy that allows the body to move with a natural, unforced strength. To have smooth, flowing movements requires a calm spirit, tranquil heart, and concentration of mind. Relaxation, clarity of feeling, and attention are essential. Spirit and thought are gathered internally and concentrated within oneself. The prime mover is the mind, but the movement is propelled by Chi. The mind directs the Chi to move the body. If you steer the Chi with the mind, Chi will lead the blood. Whichever part of the body is being concentrated on becomes positive, Yang. By relaxing the muscles, blood is allowed to flow freely under the guidance of chi. There should be no strain or tension in the shoulders or arms. Keep a calm facial expression.

By focusing on moving in accordance with nature, the student develops both skill and concentration. The mental chattering of the mind becomes still. It takes concentration and focus to be able to learn and memorize the complex sequence of physical movements. The student must have an awareness of the body and its movements, and focus on making movements sustained and flowing with no pauses, jerkiness, or force. One should make the movements as quiet and peaceful as possible, with the quiet originating from an internal point at the center of the body that expands outward. The energy flows from this point inside, radiating outward through arms, legs, and head. The thirteen movements of Tai-Chi Chuan signify ways in which foot and hand motions are integrated as they emerge from the body's center. They represent thirteen *methods* of movement rather than thirteen particular actions.

The movements demand naturalness; they should not be forced. Every movement must involve the entire body. The whole body moves lightly, nimbly, and in coordination, with no uneven distribution or discontinuity. Move the right side and left side, and the arms and legs, simultaneously.

The body should remain centered and comfortable, able to handle impact from any direction. Keep the body erect, with the center of the waist and top of the head in a straight line, no leaning to sides. The strength is developed from the vertebrae, while the spine and waist are the source of power. The body is poised like a hawk ready to pounce on a rabbit; the spirit is alert like a cat about to surprise a mouse.

The conception of Tai-Chi as the union of Yang and Yin can be seen in the basic advice given to students of the Tai-Chi Chuan art. One's movements are to be "not too slow, not too fast; not too hard, not too soft." In short, the movements of Tai-Chi Chuan are balanced, with a relaxed tempo, no hurry, no slack. The speed of movements remains even; advance and retreat are easily interchangeable.

The movement is said to "have its root in the feet, be controlled by the waist, and expressed by the fingers" (Sifu).

The feet should be straight, not pigeon-toed or bow-legged. Steps should be neither too small nor too far apart, and should be nimble, with the agility of a cat. The steps follow the revolving body; the body turns and the steps follow. When retreating or advancing, step first, and the body follows.

FIGURE IV.3: *Students from Tien-Jin City, China, perform Step Back and Repulse Monkey.*

Normally, the body's weight is carried equally by both legs. But in Tai-Chi Chuan, the body's weight is supported by one leg at a time. The supporting leg is positive (Yang) and supports the weight of the body; the empty, negative (Yin) leg must be able to be moved easily. It is necessary to be aware of weight shifting from one leg to another, with every step being lively, firm, and powerful. One must be able to distinguish Yin and Yang, hollow and solid legs, at all times. If weight is divided between legs, then the attention will be divided. The focus should always be on one at a time.

The chest should not protrude. The back should be straight, with the coccyx (small bone at base of spine) and lowest segments of vertebrae kept in central position in relation to gravity.

Breathe long and deep from the tan-tien. Let the Chi sink. The center should be comfortable and at ease. Loosen the pelvic muscles, and have no tension in the abdomen. The waist is the center of all bodily movement. As strength radiates from the waist, it descends through the legs into the feet, and rises through the torso into shoulders, arms, and hands.

One must sink to strike. When pushing or pulling, strength comes from the spine.

Hold the head as though it were suspended from the top by a string, or as though balancing something on top of it. The head does not move forward or back, nor from side to side. Keep a lively spirit, with eyes fixed straight ahead, at eye level. The top energy is empty and light, representing the Yang half of the body. Use the mind while practicing the movements to develop mental control as well as physical coordination. This involves clearing the mind and allowing a quietness to settle in, so that within this quietness, the mind can rest and concentrate at the same time. The concentration must be 100 percent on the Tai-Chi Chuan form, with awareness of the whole body, but focusing on certain, specific areas with each movement. Practicing Tai-Chi Chuan provides mental exercise, increasing powers of concentration and developing mental control over physical movements.

When there is no motion, you are still as a mountain; when moving, be as fluid and as mutable as water. Whenever there is motion, Yin and Yang separate; whenever there is stillness, Yin and Yang recombine. Patience is a very important aspect of fruitful practice. When the practitioner of Tai-Chi Chuan becomes preoccupied with the grace of the movements, there is a tendency not to execute the moves completely. It is vital to complete each move fully. Grace will come naturally with diligent daily practice. Keep Chi circulating freely through the whole body, letting it penetrate to the bones. When the Chi has circulated throughout the entire body, call it a round of exercise.

One should always be aware of the breath while practicing. Respirations become long and deep from the tan-tien as the vitality is aroused. The breathing should be kept calm and natural, inhaling and exhaling into the center, where the body's dualities are harmonized. The attention is placed in the center of the body, where all of the complementary Yin-Yang aspects of the body meet and reverse polarities.

With continuous practice, the student learns to make all movements from this balanced center, allowing the universal energies to issue forth from their internal Tai-Chi state, coming to deeper understanding and experience of these forces within and around us. This knowledge can be put into use when these same energies manifest in the various events and environments of our day-to-day life, putting the Tai-Chi student in a position to act in a harmonizing way.

Tai-Chi Chuan is a lifetime learning process. It opens communication between your mind and your body, which is beneficial to mental and physical health and can facilitate more open lines of communication to the natural world, in your relationships, and especially to your teacher. Personal practice connects you to inner virtues, which you must discover and cultivate for yourself: integrity, respect, appreciation, honesty, humility, attention, courage, and confidence.

Proper practice can produce skillfulness.

To teach your body what to do is a very difficult feat that takes great patience and humility. Communication between the mind and body brings a glow to the soul. As a conditioning exercise for the body, Tai-Chi Chuan is a non-strenuous form of exercise that stretches and strengthens the muscles, improves circulation and respiratory capacities, and quickens reflexes. There are many practical benefits, such as improved balance and a new sense of grace in movements. Its renowned health benefits—energy and flexibility, inner strength and concentration—are grounded in the deep understanding of human nature at the core of Chinese philosophy.

FIGURE IV.4: *Blind student Lin Hsueh-Chin performs Tai-Chi Chuan.*

Although today the self-defense aspect is not generally emphasized, Tai-Chi Chuan was originally developed as a form of martial arts. As a technique for self-defense, Tai-Chi Chuan is unique because of its emphasis on mental cultivation and spiritual training rather than physical force and muscular development. The idea is to overcome an opponent by absorbing his force and—through tranquility of movement—turn the attacker's own strength against him. The general principles behind Tai-Chi Chuan as a martial art are "non-aggression" and "non-resistance." The goal is more a mental state than a physical condition. The even tempo and unforced movements of Tai-Chi Chuan—which do not seem to have any relationship to the hard, swift movements normally associated with self-defense—teach a student how to use mental concentration and spiritual calm to defend against physical assault. Even though Tai-Chi Chuan was developed as a very sophisticated self-defense system, today it is practiced almost solely as a method of physical and mental conditioning, and not as a martial art.

Nevertheless, in learning the Tai-Chi Chuan form, self-defense technique is automatically developed through a greater awareness of the body and of one's physical space. By calming the mind and emotions, one is able to act composedly in any situation that may arise, combining mental stillness with physical swiftness. Yet this faculty can only be cultivated through internal discipline.

Martial Arts Weapons

In addition to being a system of self-cultivation that creates deep physical and psychological benefits, Tai-Chi Chuan is a form of self-defense based upon awareness. Traditional practice of the art has, therefore, often included training in the use of weapons, as well as in push-hands—with an eye toward activating and exploring forms of movement and awareness that may be encountered in face-to-face combat. In each dynasty, new martial arts weapons were created and old ones discarded. Thus the Chinese martial arts weapons have evolved through many centuries.

With the development of modern weapons technology, it is true that much of the fiercest combat has become utterly impersonal … and no longer face to face.

Struggle is, nevertheless, inherent in life on this Earth—and self-awareness in the context of combat can only increase the student's ability to thrive … and to make peace within him- or herself as well as within situations of conflict encountered in the world.

FIGURE IV.5: *Student Chris Reed performs Tai Chi Chuan sword.*

FIGURE IV.6: *Tamar Margolit performs Shao-Lin broadsword, single sword style.*

Three Steps to Learning Tai-Chi Chuan

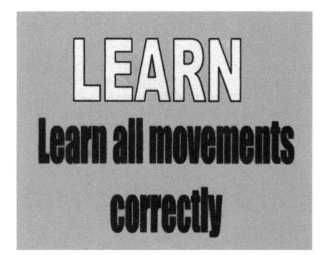

LEARN
Learn all movements correctly

PRACTICE
Practice what you learn and memorize until it comes naturally

CULTIVATE
Cultivate to become graceful and develop skill

Correct Tai-Chi Chuan Form

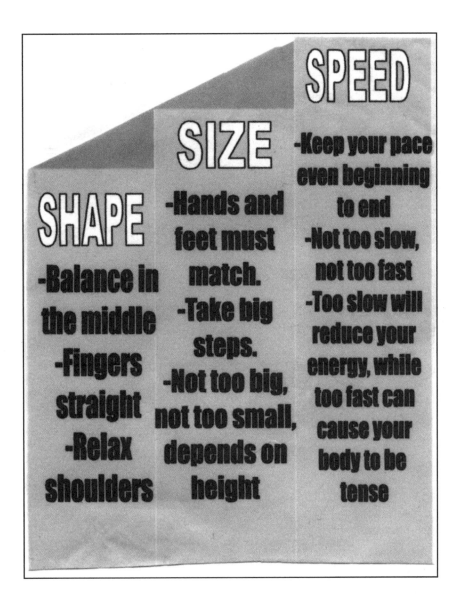

(Designed by Joe Moran)

Chin-to-Toe

The chin-to-toe exercise is a gateway to the great benefits of Tai-Chi Chuan. Traditionally, in China, a prospective student was required to perform the difficult chin-to-toe exercise before even beginning to learn the movements of the Tai-Chi Chuan form. This was the lineage's way of protecting its teachers from wasting time with students who weren't serious. Even in the context of modern culture, Simu Kuo requires that students who wish to teach put their chin to toe.

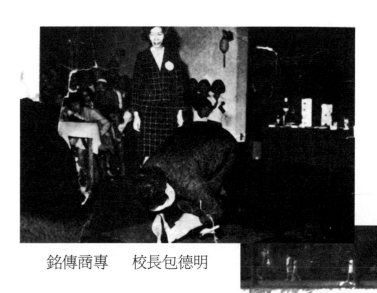

楊志芳

銘傳商專　校長包德明

FIGURE IV.7: *In the old days, the Chinese teacher expected the student to perform chin-to-toe before he or she could begin learning the Tai-Chi Chuan form.*

The practice of the chin-to-toe exercise engages the whole being: strengthening and stretching the entire body, head to foot, especially the psoas muscles, which knit the leg bones to the pelvis and spine. The spine itself opens and stretches. All this results in improved circulation and flexibility, while expanding the breath and directing it from the muscles and tendons into the subtle systems of the inner organs, and cardiovascular, skeletal, and central nervous systems. It also increases the ability to perform high kicks while maintaining stillness in the upper body.

The exercise has other important aspects as well. It puts one in the position of struggling to accomplish something one never imagined possible. For individuals who are already well stretched out, this aspect may not pertain, since they may put chin to toe within a matter of months, or even weeks. For others, though, it may take unwavering persistence over a period of years. In the process, a tremendous amount is learned: how to make the right kind of effort (not too hard, not too soft), how to make an effort without being attached to the result, and how to move slowly toward what seems like an unattainable goal. In attempting this stretch, we come up against the intensity of our ambition and impatience. Students often complain, at least inwardly, about the difficulty of the exercise; yet it is precisely this difficulty that provides an inexhaustible opportunity for the development of will—embodied will—that harnesses all one's strength, soul force, and concentration in a single action, toward a single goal. Undertaking a practice that may take a couple of years to complete stabilizes the personality, bringing latent "defects" to the surface, forcing the practitioner to slowly bring every aspect of him- or herself into the arena. And not just the good boy or good girl parts, but also the surly and lazy parts, the impatient parts, the parts that, perhaps in the past, have always given up when the going got rough. There's also a symbolism to the effort to put chin to toe, not dissimilar to the symbolism involved in doing prostrations: rather than focusing on flights of fantasy, one is brought back, over and over again, to the body, to the earth, as the Yang upper body is lowered to the Yin lower body. In the process, it is necessary both to accept and to struggle against one's very apparent limitations. Nothing could be more humbling, nothing more edifying. The powers of human intention and motivation are truly great: it's always a question of how much we wish for something, and of what sacrifices we are willing to make in order to bring it about.

For this reason, anyone can reap great benefits from practicing this exercise diligently, whether or not the chin ever reaches the toe. What's needed most of all is to find a way, day after day, of putting one's heart into the practice, and making the right kind of effort—not too hard, not too soft. It is an extremely gradual process, which can only succeed if one gets into long, slow, smooth breathing. The exercise is very humbling: slowly stretching the upper part of the body all the way down to the lower. The Yang force of awareness is carefully directed into the substance of the body, which is Yin. The result of this process is the steady growth of patience, inner strength, and balance—the essence of Tai-Chi.

Daily practice involves continuous self-refinement, or "sweeping the heart." By making the effort to renew aspiration over and again, we keep moving in the direction of real wholeness. This is a living, ever-changing wholeness, which includes all the different aspects of our being in vital connection with the world around us.

The Lien-Ying Tai-Chi Chuan Academy is happy to present these students for mastering the chin-to-toe exercise:

Simmone Kuo	June Y. Chung	Mei Kuo
Judy Job	Jeffrey Kessler	Bill Varela
Barbara Riddle Cellers	Chris Reed	Benoit D'aures
Eric Paul Shaber	Phil Greven	Bell Zeidman
Chiu Yee Ming	Dian	Sam Williams
Danny Kent	Saiyong	Shannon Cook
Peter Hensill	Sheng Zhen-Shen	Denton Liversparger
Tyler Francis	Liu Tsen Duh	Karen
Chen Dong-Feng	Hieu Ha	Roger Taylor
John Bendrick	Chang Fong	Manvil Basco
Paula	Solomon Russell	Jacob Aringo
Marietta Arroyo	Damian Alvarado	Serena Chew
Lisa Rasmussen	Kyoshi Mana	Tim McAuliffe
Heidi Thomas		

Chin-to-Toe

Teaching Tai-Chi Chuan

FIGURE IV.8: *The teacher sometimes corrects the student hand to hand to ensure that she is performing the moves correctly.*

For the study of Tai-Chi Chuan, a good teacher is hard to find, but a good student is also hard to find. A good teacher never has any expectations, and in that way she never gets disappointed. The teachers themselves practice every day and give encouragement to their students. Yet they do not overencourage them, push them too hard, or stroke their egos. Never tell students that they are "very good" because the "devil"—forces of negativity such as overconfidence and complacency—might get in the way of good practice. The strength of Tai-Chi Chuan can bring great confidence, but it is not to be used against others or to feel pleasure in knocking others down. This kind of behavior is ungrateful and will cause students to forget the movements of the form.

FIGURE IV.9: *Sifu explains to the student, "Practicing Tai-Chi Chuan is like eating a meal, you must do it every day. Time and the seasons are never late, they will not wait for you. You must earn your good health, which is a benefit to you, your family, society, and the country."*

師傅說： "歲月不饒人,季節不讓人. 身體練好, 對家庭, 社會, 國家都好."

練拳與食飯一樣, 每天食飯, 每天練拳.

Tai-Chi Chuan from the earliest times has been used not only as physical exercise, but also as a means to keep the practitioner mentally alert and emotionally calm. This aspect of Tai-Chi Chuan can be introduced into physical education curricula for the purpose of teaching students a technique for relaxation and concentration. Instead of focusing on the conditioning aspects of the movements, the teacher encourages the students to concentrate on moving in particular ways and on being aware of particular mental images while practicing the sets. Focusing on these images and movement qualities helps the students to develop a disciplined concentration, which in turn produces a mental and emotional equilibrium, calmness, and alertness.

During a basic Tai-Chi Chuan course, the main objectives are to have the students experience the following processes:

- Learn a non-strenuous form of exercise
- Learn a traditional Chinese approach to holistic fitness, emphasizing the conditioning of the whole person including the mind, body, and spirit
- Be exposed to the notion of a non-aggressive form of martial art

Tai-Chi Chuan can also be included in sports, gymnastics, or dance programs. The emphasis in this approach is on Tai-Chi Chuan as a conditioning for the body or as a warm-up for physical activities. Tai-Chi Chuan develops strength, control, flexibility, and balance—all of which are needed for athletic activities and events. Employed at the beginning of a class, the Tai-Chi Chuan form and exercises loosen, limber, warm up, and calm the students as they perform the quiet movements. If it is practiced at the end of a strenuous class, it helps the students to gain control of their tired bodies and excited emotions. In either case, utilizing Tai-Chi Chuan practice for 10 or 15 minutes in the class benefits both student and teacher.

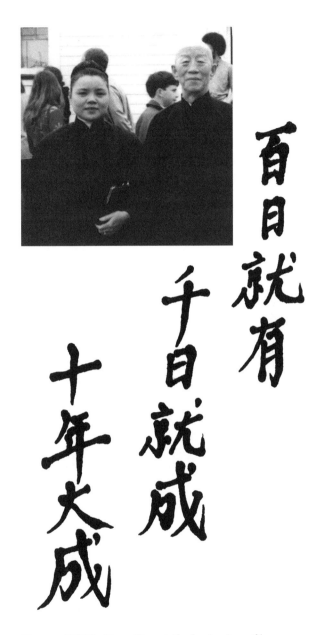

百日就有
千日就成
十年大成

FIGURE IV.10: *Simu Kuo at the beginning of her career; Sifu Kuo at the end of his....*

It takes 100 days to plant the seeds, 1,000 days for the seeds to bear fruit, and 10,000 days for the fruit to ripen. This is a metaphor for the discipline and results of Tai-Chi Chuan.

V

Yin-Yang in Society and the Cultural Arts: Chinese Literature

It is important that students of Tai-Chi Chuan also study philosophy and cultural arts, so that the mind grows in understanding and the heart in goodness, as the body gains in strength and flexibility. Here, too, the focus is on balancing of the Yin-Yang energies. To discipline the body without also training the mind and spirit could leave the student unbalanced, even violent. Reading poetry and philosophy helps to stabilize the mind and feed the heart, so that the student can participate effectively and harmoniously in society.

In traditional China, after a martial arts teacher got to know a student, the student would sometimes be invited into the teacher's home, to share meals and swap stories like a member of the family. Sifu Kuo followed this method with his students: he loved to tell teaching stories, and often used poetry or philosophical aphorisms to illustrate his ideas.

This section of the book presents a potpourri of Sifu's favorite Chinese literature and philosophy. Wu Shu, the great martial arts tradition of China grew out the blending of Taoist and Confucian streams of thought. Therefore, I've included material from philosophers from both traditions. Lao Tzu was the original philosopher of the Tao, while Mencius was a great scholar in the generation after Confucius, and was the author of one of the Four Classics of the Confucian canon.

Later, when Buddhism came to China (in the first century c.e.), it also became an important influence on the practice and teaching of martial arts. This is why I've included a brief section on the Monkey King, the famous Beijing Opera that chronicles a Buddhist monk's pilgrimage from China back to India—the source of Buddhism—accompanied by three fabulous martial artists in animal form. In addition, you'll find a selection of the Tang poetry Sifu favored for its feelingful portrayals of the natural world. The section concludes with a number of aphorisms and traditional teaching parables based on events in Chinese history.

Throughout, I've selected material Sifu enjoyed. Try reading a passage before going out to practice, and let it speak in your heart while your mind becomes still.

Lao Tzu and the *Tao Te Ching*

The traditional philosophy of China, from prehistoric times, involved following the Tao, or the natural way of things. Taoism only arose as a religious sect to contrast Confucianism. The legendary Lao Tzu, reputed founder of Taoism, is said to have been born under unusual circumstances in Honan in the seventh century B.C.E. Some legends say he was immaculately conceived to a shooting star. It is also said that he was carried in his mother's womb for sixty to eighty years before birth, and was therefore born with white hair (in 604 B.C.E.), hence the name *Lao Tzu*, meaning "Fully Mature." He is most famous for a collection of his writings known as the *Tao Te Ching*.

As Lao Tzu made ready to leave society and wander in the wilderness, the guard at the city gate would not allow him to leave unless he left some of his renowned wisdom for later generations. Lao Tzu then wrote 5,000 Chinese characters in eighty-one short chapters that would become the *Tao Te Ching* and retreated from the world. Some legends say that he left China, and the time and place of his death are unknown; others say he died and is buried in China. One story is that he traveled to India and there became the legendary teacher of Siddhartha Gautama, the Buddha. And still other traditions claim that Lao Tzu was immortal.

Lao Tzu taught that men should live naturally, in harmony with their environment, without striving, contrivance, or scheming. "Never interfere, and let things take their natural course" was his doctrine. He himself did not consider Taoism a religion, but simply a way of understanding how the world around him operated. Later, his teachings were preached, and he himself was revered as a saint.

Verses from the Tao Te Ching

The Tao gives birth to One,
One gives birth to yin and yang,
Yin and yang give birth to all things.
Being and non-being produce each other;
Difficulty and ease complete each other;
Long and short contrast each other;
High and low distinguish each other;
Sound and voice harmonize each other;
Front and back follow each other.

天地相合, 以降甘露,
民莫之令而自均.
始制有名, 名亦即有,
夫亦將知止, 知止所以不殆.
璧道之在天下, 猶川谷之與江海.

The Heaven and Earth join,
    And the sweet rain falls,
Beyond command of men, yet evenly upon all.

Then human civilization arose and there were names.
Since there were names,
    It were well no one knew where to stop.
He who knows where to stop
    May be exempt from danger.
Tao in the world
    May be compared to rivers that run into the sea.

老子
我有三寶, 持而保之.
一曰慈, 二曰儉, 三曰不敢爲天下先.
慈故能勇, 儉故能廣, 不敢爲天下先, 故能成器長.

I have Three Treasures;
Guard them and keep them safe:
    The first is Love.
    The second is, Never too much.
    The third is, Never be the first in the world.
Through Love, one has no fear;
Through not doing too much, one has a plentitude
        (of reserve power);
Through not presuming to be first in the world,
    One can develop one's talent and let it mature.

老 子

持而盈之, 不如其巳;
揣而鋭之, 不可長保.
金玉満堂, 默之能守;
富貴而驕, 自遺其咎.
功成身退, 天之道.

Stretch (a bow) to the very full,
  And you will wish you had stopped in time.
Temper a (sword-edge) to its very sharpest,
  And the edge will not last long.
When gold and jade fill your hall,
  You will not be able to keep them safe.
To be proud of wealth and honor
  Is to sow the seeds of one's own downfall.
Retire when work is done,
  Such is Heaven's way.

Mencius and Book Four of the Four Chinese Classics

Mencius was one of the premier Chinese philosophers, whose writings form the fourth of the Four Books of the Chinese classics. He was an ardent supporter of Confucianism, but he studied human nature from the point of view of political economy.

He was born in the State of Tsou (鄒), in modern Shantung, in B.C.E. 372. The formation of his character was chiefly due to his mother, to whose sole care he devolved upon the untimely death of his father. He held office as Minister under Prince Hsüan of Ch'i State at the age of 45, but subsequently retired into private life and devoted the remainder of his days to literary pursuits.

His tablet is placed in the Confucian temples.

FIGURE V.2: *Mencius* (孟子)

Though the entire *Tao Te Ching* is contained in a slim volume, the Four Books or Four Classics of the Confucian canon are lengthy, detailed, and dense. The Four Classics form the basis for much of traditional East Asian culture and society—not only in China, but also in Korea, Japan, and Southeast Asia. Most important are the *Analects* of Confucius himself.

If a man takes no thought about what is distant
He will find sorrow near at hand

—CONFUCIUS

The middle books are entitled *The Great Learning* and *The Doctrine of the Mean*. In these, the dynamics of Yin-Yang are discussed with respect to history, philosophy, and the natural world. In the fourth and last book, *The Works of Mencius*, the ethical teachings of Confucius are clarified and applied to daily life. Mencius's discussion of correct, hierarchical relationships—with their emphasis on mutual respect and caring—is of particular significance to martial arts practice, where the teacher-student relationship is of primary importance for the transmission of skill and knowledge.

Mencius was a student of the students of Confucius, but his greatest teacher was his own mother. In their relationship, both mother and son fulfilled their roles with great diligence. Later generations have honored Mencius's mother for her devoted parenting and Mencius himself as an exemplar of filial piety.

Mencius's mother moved three times to bring her son to an area with a good school for him to learn in, but each time he failed to engage himself in his studies. Finally, Mencius's mother broke the loom that she worked on to make an example to him: he too will be useless for work if he does not apply himself. This made him understand the error of his ways, after which he apologized and promised to be a useful, responsible citizen.

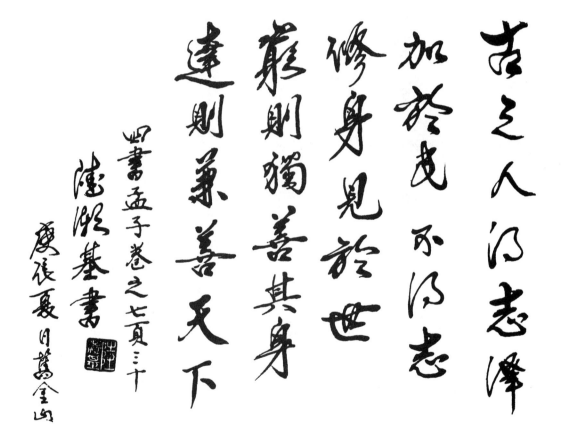

"When the men of antiquity realized their wishes, benefits were conferred by them on the people. If they did not realize their wishes, they cultivated their personal character, and became illustrious in the world. If poor, they attended to their own virtue in solitude; if advanced to dignity, they made the whole empire virtuous as well."

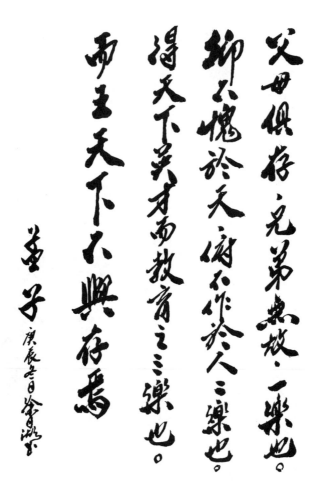

Three Delights

1. That his father and mother are both alive and that the condition of his brothers affords no cause for anxiety;—this is one delight.

2. That when looking up he has no occasion of shame before heaven, and when looking below he has no occasion to blush before men;—this is a second delight.

3. That he can get from the whole empire the most talented individuals and teach and nourish them; — that is a third delight.

The superior man has three things in which he delights, and to be ruler over the empire is not one of them.

*What belongs by his nature to the superior man are benevolence,
righteousness, propriety, and knowledge.*

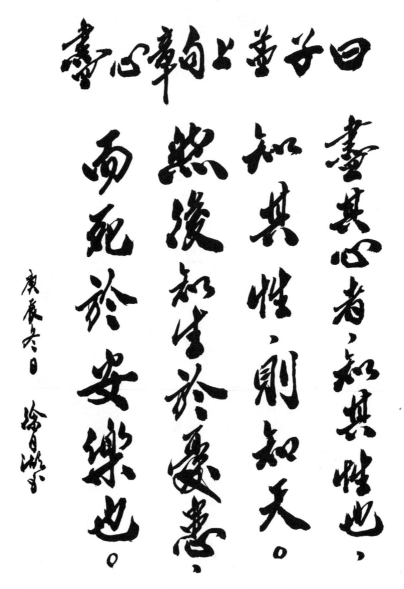

These are rooted in his heart; their growth and manifestation are a mild harmony appearing in the countenance, a rich fullness in the back, and the character imparted to the four limbs. Those limbs understand to arrange themselves without being told.

Mencius said, "He who has exhausted all his mental constitution knows his nature. Knowing his nature, he knows heaven."

"From these things we see how life springs from sorrow and calamity, and death from ease and pleasure."

—All quotes from *The Four Books: Confucian Analects, The Great Learning, The Doctrine of the Mean, The Works of Mencius*, TRANS. JAMES LEGGE

The Monkey King

FIGURE V.3: *The Monkey King is renowned for its spectacular martial arts fighting scenes, in which a variety of traditional weapons is used with amazing dexterity. Here the Monkey King prepares to strike with his magical staff.*

"The Monkey King: Journey to the West" is a traditional story in the Beijing Opera, based on Hsuan-Tsang's (594–664 C.E.) famous pilgrimage. It tells of the redemption of a high official who has made some serious life mistakes. Through his dedication to his Master, he redeems himself and regains his humility. The story is called Journey to the West because its many incidents take place in the course of the pilgrimage of an early Chinese Buddhist back to India, in search of more teaching sutras. The pilgrimage is an allegory of the taming and transformation of selfish impulses, via dedication to the dharma, the great Buddhist teaching.

FIGURE V.4: *Here the Buddhist pilgrim is depicted with his disciples—Monkey King, Pig, and Fish—who represent the ego's pride, greed, and fearfulness. (From Monkey King Subdues the White Bone Demon, adapted by Hsing-pei. Drawing by Chao Hung-pin and Chien Hsiao-taI. Beijing: Foreign Languages Press, 1976.)*

Chinese Poems of the Tang Dynasty

唐诗三百首新译

古人曰：
詩爲樂心，聲爲樂體

*Poetry and music bring contentment to the
human body and mind.*

Chinese poetry flourished during the Tang Dynasty (618–907 C.E.). Sifu particularly valued Tang poetry for its spare yet evocative descriptions of the Chinese landscape. The heightened appreciation for the cyclical patterns and awesome beauty of the natural world typically leads the Tang poet into reflections on the place of human beings within the natural order.

A similar fusion of the natural world with the inner world is one of the hallmarks of successful Tai-Chi Chuan practice. This is why it is best to practice Tai-Chi Chuan outdoors, if possible, where the air is fresh and the earth and sky are visible. The goal of practice is to bring oneself into balance not as an isolated individual, but as a living embodiment of the Yin-Yang energies, which are creating and sustaining the entire world.

Mooring at Dusk

夕次盱眙縣　　　　韋應物
落帆逗淮鎮, 停舫臨孤驛.
浩浩風起波, 冥冥日沈夕.
人歸山郭暗, 雁下蘆洲白.
獨夜憶秦關, 聽鐘未眠客.

Mooring at Dusk in Xuyi County

Wei Yingwu

Dropping sail at a county on the Huai,
　　My boat lies near a vacant courier's rest.
The winds from shore to shore the waters ruffle;
　　Dimly, dimly sinks the sun in the west.
The hillside town, deserted now, looms dark;
　　The wild geese 'lighted, the reedy isle gleams white.
With thoughts on home, a sleepless traveller
　　Is counting the bells—through this lonley night.

Song of Roamer

遊子吟　　　　　孟郊
慈母手中線, 遊子身上衣.
臨行密密縫, 意恐遲遲歸!
誰言春草心, 報得三春輝?

Song of Roamer

Meng Jiao

The threads in a kind mother's hand—
A gown for her son bound for far-off land,
Sewn stitch by stitch before he leaves
　　For fear his return be delayed.
Such kindness as young grass receives
　　From the warm sun can't be repaid.

To Hermit Wei, the Eighth among His Brothers

贈衛八處士　　　　杜甫
人生不相見, 動如參與商; 今夕復何夕, 共此燈燭光.
少壯能幾時, 鬢髮各已蒼. 訪舊半爲鬼, 驚乎熱中腸.
焉知二十載, 重上君子堂, 昔別君未昏, 兒女忽成行!
怡然敬父執, 問我來何方? 問答乃未已, 驅兒羅酒漿.
夜雨剪春韭, 新炊間黃粱. 主稱會面難, 一舉累十觴,
十觴亦不醉, 感子故意長! 明日隔山岳, 世事兩茫茫!

To Hermit Wei, the Eighth among His Brothers

Du Fu

How rarely in life do we meet together,
Morning and Evening Stars too, miss each other.
Ah, what a happy night it is tonight,
We sit, face to face, in the candle light!
How many days one can claim young and sound?
On our temples much grey hair can be found.
Half of our friends have given up the ghost,
I cry, when I visit them, my bowels roast.
I never expected twenty years have fled
Before I come again to your homestead.
You were unmarried the day I left erstwhile,
Your sons and daughters now stand in a file.
They gladly greet their father's bosom friend,
And ask me if I've come from a strange land.
We are busy in our conversation
While wine and all are in preparation.
The leeks are cut in the spring night, raining;
The meal with yellow millet is hot steaming.
My host says it is very hard to meet,
Raising ten times his goblet to greet.
It does not make me drunk even quaffing ten,
Owing to my grateful heart I can sustain.
Tomorrow, betwixt us the mountain will intrude;
We'll each be lost in the vastness of the world!

(translated by Wu Juntao)

The Red Cliff
by Su Tung Po

念奴嬌　蘇軾

大江東去浪淘盡，千古風流人物，故壘西邊

人道是三國周郎赤壁，亂石崩雲驚

濤裂岸，捲起千堆雪，江山如畫，一時多

少豪傑。

遙想公瑾當年，小喬初嫁了，雄姿英發，

羽扇綸巾，談笑間，強虜灰飛煙滅，故

國神遊，多情應笑我，早生華髮，人

間如夢，一尊還酹江月。

The Red Cliff
by Su Tung Po

The River flows to the East
Its waves have washed away all
The heroes of history.
To the West of the ancient
Wall you enter the Red Gorge
Of Chu Ko Liang of the
Days of the three Kingdoms.
The jagged peaks pierce the heavens.
The furious rapids beat
At the boat, and dash up in
A thousand clouds of spray
Like snow. Mountain and river
Have often been painted,
In the memory of the heroes
Of those days. I remember

Long ago, Kung Ch'in newly
Married to the beautiful
Chiao-siao, shining in splendor,
A young warrior, and the other
Chu Ko Liang, in his blue cap,
Waving his horsetail duster,
Smiling and chatting as he
Burned the navy of Ts'ao Ts'ao.
Their ashes were scattered to
The Four Winds. They vanished away
In smoke. I like to dream of
Those dead kingdoms. Let people
Laugh at my prematurely
Grey hair. My answer is
A wine cup, full of the
Moon drowned in the River.

From Kenneth Rexroth, One Hundred Poems from the Chinese

From Three Kingdoms

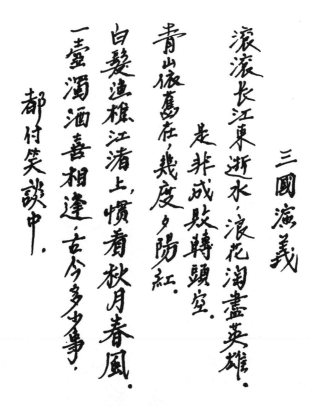

滾滾長江東逝水，浪花淘盡英雄。

是非成敗轉頭空。

青山依舊在，幾度夕陽紅。

白髮漁樵江渚上，慣看秋月春風。

一壺濁酒喜相逢，古今多少事，

都付笑談中。

三國演義

From Three Kingdoms

The Long River passes east away
Surge over surge,
Whiteblooming waves sweep all heroes on
As right and wrong, triumph and defeat all turn unreal.
But ever the green hills stay
To blush in the west-waning day.

The woodcutters and the fishermen,
Whiteheaded, they've seen enough
Spring air and autumn moon
To make good company over the winejars,
Where many a famed event
Provides their merriement.

(translated by Moss Roberts)

Snow

沁園春雪　　　一九三六年二月
北國風光, 千里冰封, 萬里雪飄.
望長城內外, 惟餘莽莽; 大河上下, 頓失滔滔.
山舞銀蛇, 原馳蠟象, 欲與天公試比高.
須晴日, 看紅裝素裹, 分外妖嬈.
江山如此比嬌, 引無數文采; 唐宗宋祖, 稍孫風騷.
一代天驕, 成吉思汗, 只識彎弓射大雕.
俱往矣, 數風流人物, 還看今朝.

Snow

to the tune of Chin Yuan Chun, February, 1936

North country scene:
A hundred leagues locked in ice,
A thousand leagues of whirling snow.
Both sides of the Great Wall
One single white immensity.
The Yellow River's swift current
Is still from end to end.
The mountains dance like silver snakes
and the highlands* charge like wax-hued elephants,
Vying with heaven in stature.
On a fine day, the land,
Clad in white, adorned in red,
Grows more enchanting.

This land so rich in beauty
Has made countless heroes bow in homage.
But alas! Chin Shih-huang and Han Wu-ti

Were lacking in literary grace,
And Tang Tai-tsung and Sung Tai-tsu
Had little poetry in their souls;
And Ghengis Khan,
Proud Son of Heaven for a day,
Knew only shooting eagles, bow oustretched.
All are past and gone
For truly great men
Look to this age alone.

*AUTHOR'S NOTE: *The highlands are those of Shensi and Shansi*

Chinese Aphorisms

Learning Builds the Foundation of Enrichment
Working Hard Is the Source of Prosperity

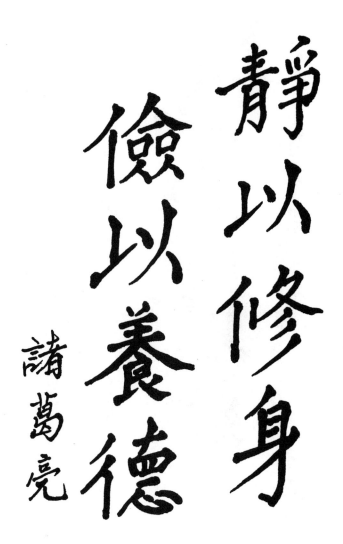

A steel will rebuilds strength.
No waste will maintain prosperity and attain virtue.

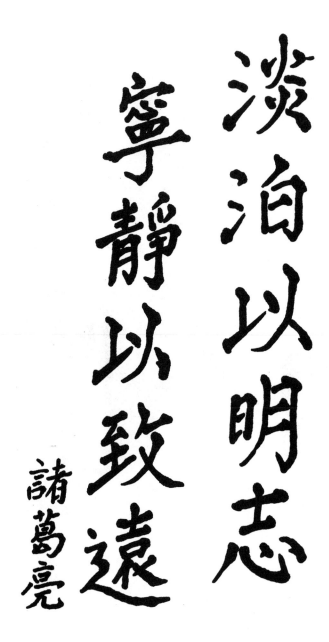

Clarity comes from still dispassion;
Long-term resolution from quiet concentration.

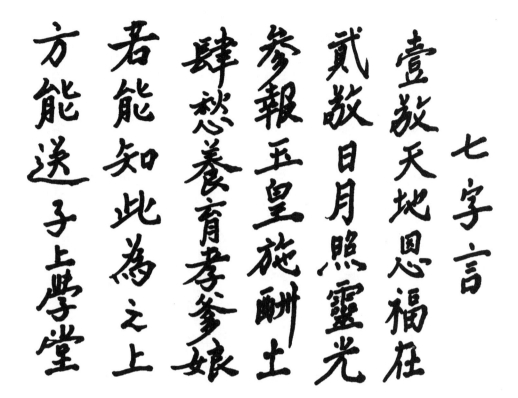

七字言

壹 敬 天 地 恩 福 在
貳 敬 日 月 照 靈 光
參 報 五 皇 施 酬 土
肆 愁 養 育 孝 爹 娘
君 能 知 此 為 之 上
方 能 送 子 上 學 堂

Thank heaven and earth for the blessing
Thank sun and moon for the enlightenment
Thank god for the abundance
Thank parents for the nourishment
Only when you know how to thank
Before we send our children to school.

Chinese Parables

(Chinese characters written by LAWRENCE P. LUI*)*

In the Chinese martial arts tradition, much of the moral teaching is done indirectly, by means of stories. The following teaching parables are all based on famous incidents in Chinese history. Each parable is used to illustrate one of the traditional Confucian virtues. Such moral teaching forms an essential part of martial arts training, whose goal is the creation of strong human beings, who are also wise, compassionate, and committed to creating a just society.

The Law of Propriety: Confucius's Inquiry

Confucius (551–479 B.C.E.), the teacher of all ages in China, attached great importance to the law of propriety as one of the cardinal virtues in his entire ethical system. *Li* (propriety) is both the principle of personal conduct and the essence of social, moral, and religious practices. After making an exhaustive study of the cultural heritages of the three preceding dynasties, Confucius is said to have taken a trip to see Lao Tzu, the earliest Chinese philosopher and founder of Taoism, for his views of *Li*. This marks Confucius as a man of humility and learning, the father of *Li*.

禮

孔子問禮

百世之師孔子, 生時對於夏殷周三代禮儀當作實地考證, 擬增刪損益, 酌中重訂, 禮是立身處世之道, 也是文化制度之本. 孔子固此當不達千里就教於老子, 這種敬老尊賢, 慮心向學的精神, 使孔子本身爲中國禮的代表.

Righteousness: Eternal Friendship in the Peach Garden

Liu Pei, the ruler of the Kingdom of Shu at the time of the Three Kingdoms (221–265 C.E.), is represented in the Chinese historical romance as the incarnation of the everlasting friendship that existed between his two faithful followers, Chang Fei and Kuan Yu. The three took a solemn oath of eternal friendship and allegiance as sworn brothers in the peach garden and worked together in the establishment of their kingdom. Sworn brotherhood has since then been popular among the Chinese; Kuan Yu, the most celebrated of all generals of the time, was later deified as a god of war.

義

桃園結義

漢末劉氏後裔劉憊, 寬厚弘毅, 喜結交天下莫豪, 與關羽張飛在桃園結義, 當指天設誓, 有福同享, 有難同當, 三人雖非同生, 但願同死, 後來共劍大業, 劉氏被奉爲蜀主, 與魏吳鼎足而立, 號稱三國, 而劉關張三人道義之交, 世皆傳誦.

Integrity: Yang Chen's Four Knows

Wang Mi, who had been appointed magistrate through his recommendation, one evening offered Yang Chen a handsome bribe in gold. "It's dark here and no one will know about this," Wang said. "No one knows?" cried out Yang Chen. "Heaven knows, earth knows. You and I also know about this!" From that time on, the ancestral hall of the Yang family has been held sacred as the "Hall of the Four Knows," and Yang Chen as the symbol of integrity. Yang was known as the Confucius of Western China. He died in 124 C.E.

廉

楊震四知

漢代的楊震, 品高節廉, 在荊州刺史任內, 曾推薦王密爲縣令, 王密感恩, 無以報答, 於是深夜推金以贈, 竟遭拒納, 王氏表示: "區區微意, 夜無人知." 楊震怒道: "天知地知, 你知我知, 何爲無知." 王羞愧無地自客, 後世尊楊震" 四知."

Sense of Shame: Sleeping on Firewood and Straw and Tasting Gall

Kou Chien, a prince of the state of Yueh, was badly defeated in the war with the state of Wu, which broke out in 496 B.C.E. He fought a retreat with the remnant of his forces to his own kingdom, where he drank from a vessel filled with gall and slept upon firewood and straw, so as to keep himself reminded of the humiliation he had suffered. After twenty years of arduous preparation and rigid discipline, Prince Kou Chien avenged himself on his enemy successfully. This historical fact has served as a morale booster to later generations under similar circumstances.

耻

臥薪嘗胆

春秋時代, 越王勾踐, 爲吳國所敗, 勾踐被擄, 替吳王夫差養馬, 受盡百般耻厚, 後獲釋歸來, 立志匡後, 於是臥薪嘗胆,不是朝夕惕厲, 經過十年出聚, 十年教訓後, 终於興兵滅吳, 雪耻復國, 越王勾踐的明耻教戰, 成爲後世激發士氣的昭示.

Filial Piety: Deer Skin for Deer Milk

Yentze of the Chou Dynasty (1122–249 B.C.E.) was too poor to buy deer milk, which was said to have a healing effect upon his mother's illness. Finally he got a deer skin, put it on, and went on all fours among a herd of deer in order to get the milk for his mother, who was miraculously cured. One day, when he was with the herd, it happened that he was nearly killed by a hunter mistaking him for a deer. For centuries, Chinese society has been founded on the time-honored family system with filial piety as the cardinal moral force.

孝
鹿皮取乳
周代的郯子, 天性至孝, 母患目疾, 家貧無力就医, 聽説乳可治目疾, 想盡方法不能得, 最後郯子披鹿皮混入鹿群中得乳, 不償失每日喂母, 母病果稍痊, 一日遇到獵人, 恐被射傷, 乃趨出告實情, 聽者都爲其孝心所動.

Brotherly Love: Bamboo Whip against a Tiger

Cheng Hankuang of the Ching Dynasty (1644–1911 B.C.E.) was born in Kiangsi Province on the eastern coast of China. He was famous for his brotherly love and the courage with which he rescued his brother from the clenching fangs of a ferocious tiger at the risk of his own life. In his boyhood, Cheng took his younger brother out to the countryside. Suddenly a tiger appeared and pounced upon the younger. It held the child in its mouth and started running. In desperation, Hankuang saved the child by whipping the beast in the head with a stick, forgetting his own danger. Brotherly love, as one of the Chinese cardinal virtues, is second only to filial piety.

悌
鞭虎求弟
清代江苏省的程含光, 少年時偕弟過出嶺, 遇虎攖弟而去, 含光急追, 用竹鞭猛擊虎頭, 虎怒拾共弟而反搏含光, 含光負弟疾奔脫險, 當時但知救弟, 心中不知有虎, 這是悌愛之至, 後來共年屆八十, 每撫竹鞭, 想到兄恩, 總是流淚.

Loyalty: Yueh Fei's Loyalty to the Country

Yueh Fei (1103–1141 C.E.) of the Sung Dynasty was greatly influenced by his father, who went without food in order to feed the hungry, and his mother, who tattooed the characters "everlasting loyalty to the country" on his back. Despite his patriotism and brilliant victory over the northern Tartars, Yueh Fei fell victim to court intrigue engineered by the treacherous prime minister Chin Kuei. As a result, he was thrown into jail and summarily executed. However, the Chinese have long remembered Yueh Fei as an embodiment of the spirit of loyalty and every literate person memorizes his heroic poems.

忠

盡忠報國

岳飛是宋代商州湯陰人, 家雖貧, 但事母至孝, 少有大志, 母姚氏在岳飛背上刺耳 "盡忠報國" 四字以勉, 當時金兵作亂, 岳飛本詔率兵直搗黄龍, 不幸奸相秦會因嬪力持和議, 用計陷害,

岳飛终於爲國損軀, 著有 "滿江红" 詞可泣可歌.

Good Faith: Chih Cha's Gift of the Sword

During the Spring and Autumn Periods (722–481 B.C.E.), Prince Chih Cha of the state of Wu had a stopover at Hsu on a worldwide fact-finding tour. He sensed the chief of state of Hsu showed great interest in his sword, but he could not part with it because he still needed it on his journey. However, he promised with all his heart to let the chief of the state have it upon his return. It happened that when his mission was over the chief of state had already passed away. Hence, he could not do otherwise but to visit the burial ground and hang the much-valued sword on a tree branch over the tomb. Perhaps it is due to his example that the Chinese person has the reputation that his word is as good as bond.

信

季子挂劍

春秋時代, 吳國太子季札, 周遊歷國, 考察氏風, 途徑徐國, 徐君慕季札所佩寶劍, 季札本欲割愛以贈, 奈因出使上獻, 但心中已默許, 擬於歸途時魎送不遲, 詎料季返抵徐國時, 徐君已死, 爲詔信用, 乃將寶劍擊徐君墓树之上而去.

路遥知馬力
日久見人心

FIGURE V.5: *This picture symbolizes how getting to know someone is like riding a horse. All may go well at first, but it is only after you have traveled a long way, endured various incidents, and come to know the horse's strengths and weaknesses that you can claim really to know the horse. So it is with a friend.*

PART 2

Practicing Tai-Chi Chuan: Student Experiences

I am including in this part of *Yin-Yang in Tai-Chi Chuan* individual essays written by some of my students, to give the reader a feeling for the great breadth and depth of experience that Tai-Chi Chuan opens up. Since these pieces were written without reference to each other, there is some repetition of ideas. Nevertheless, I think it is important to hear what students say, in their own voices. Each brings his or her special gifts, obstacles, and interests to the practice of Tai-Chi Chuan. I am proud of them all, and very grateful for their respect, passion, and dedication. May their experiences be a source of encouragement for future generations of students.

The Experience of Tai-Chi Chuan

Jeffrey Kessler
(Winter 1990–91)

One of the basic principles of the Tai-Chi philosophy of ancient China is that every experience is valuable, provided that one understands how to use it. Rather than resisting or rejecting what may, at first, seem like unfortunate circumstances, the student of Tai-Chi is encouraged to become inwardly still and open, so that he or she may respond to difficulty out of the innate flexibility and wisdom of being, rather than out of fear-based calculations of the ego.

Such reflections have been prominent in my thoughts during the past few months, as impaired physical health has dramatically altered my practice of Tai-Chi Chuan, the martial art based on China's traditional Tai-Chi philosophy. Tai Chi is an ancient philosophical idea—at least 5,000 years old—referring to the absolute or ultimate "point" of the universe that is believed to exist in all creatures. This point is understood to consist in varying balances of the two primal energies: Yin and Yang. What is known as the Yin-Yang symbol in the West is called the Tai-Chi in Chinese, for whom it is one of the many ways of expressing the idea. (Another, much more elaborate expression of the idea of Tai-Chi is contained in the system of the *Book of Changes* or *I Ching*.) Tai-Chi Chuan is the martial art (*chuan* means "fist," hence martial art) that is based on the principles of the Tai-Chi philosophy. The particular set of movements known as Tai-Chi Chuan is less than a thousand years old, although the traditions of movement from which it derives go back into pre-historical China, as does the Tai-Chi philosophy.

Three months ago, rushing about during the noon hour to unload groceries for my recently widowed father, I slipped on a wet patch of lawn and tore muscles deep within my lower abdomen and groin (severely enough so that they are still far from healed). Since I have long been accustomed to about two hours of martial arts practice every day—augmented by frequent hikes in the hills and long swims—I found it difficult to adjust to the necessity that I drastically limit my physical activity.

For the first few weeks following this injury, I alternated between states of grudging acceptance and futile attempts to force myself "to be better," to power through the pain, and so on. Then, before Thanksgiving, I suddenly became quite ill with the flu. Here, too, I pushed myself: rising to the occasion of putting on the large family Thanksgiving dinner only months after my mother's death before sinking into acute bronchitis. At this point, my energy level became so reduced that I had to give up the notion that I could or should power through, the notion that I could always "heal myself" without help from medical doctors. But, most of all, I had to give up the form of practice to which I had become both accustomed and attached. Rather than rising early and going out into the fresh air for an hour's practice, what I needed to do was to sleep in (which, for me, requires discipline!), then to stretch lightly and practice briefly indoors.

One of the first things that became clear to me, as the form of my practice was disrupted, was the extent to which I had been depending on this practice to make me feel good: It was a time to strengthen myself, to breathe deeply and rhythmically, to clear out my bloodstream, to relax my body, to flood my system with endorphins, to experience the activation and flow of deeply healing energies. Without periodic fixes (twice daily), I found myself feeling dreadful both physically and psychologically. In fact, without the self-calming effects of intensive practice, psychological conflicts (fear of death, depression, despair) soon surfaced—the same conflicts that I'd left behind almost twenty years before when I began to practice regularly.

I am not suggesting that my many years of practice amount to nothing more than a "positive" addiction. Real qualities, such as inner strength and flexibility, presence, and compassion, qualities that have a real place in the world, have been activated and, to some extent, developed. What I see is that the "power" to generate health and inner calm is limited—among other things—by my pain and my mortality, and that, like any power, it can be misused in the absence of real awareness.

After many years of practice, I find that I am more able to endure the anxieties and ambiguities of life without becoming enmeshed in rounds of samsaric reaction. (*Samsara* is the wheel of birth, death, and rebirth. It is also the wheel of karma, to which we are bound through unconsciousness and emotional reactivity.) As my health returns, and with it the inclination and the ability to practice intensively, I find myself reluctant to become overly identified with the production of enjoyable and even seemingly useful "inner states." What this experience has been teaching me is an appreciation for *relationship to the whole* as a spiritual discipline that "leaves no trace," together with a somewhat greater willingness and ability to remain in the moment—with its full array of possibilities and difficulties.

Out of 10,000 defeats, the true person fashions a single victory.
—CHUANG TZU, *"Autumn Floods"*

(Summer 2002)

The twelve years since I wrote the preceding piece have been a time for deepening practice and beginning to teach Tai-Chi Chuan on my own. I express my appreciation for Simu's strong presence, for her patience and encouragement, as I have gradually found my own direction and established a foundation for teaching. The challenge in learning to teach has been to remain grounded in the timeless essence of the art, while responding to the needs and opportunities presented by everyday life and people. In other words, the challenge has been to apply the principles of Tai-Chi philosophy in everyday life—to bring loving and conscious energy to bear on the situations I encounter.

I am grateful to both Sifu and Simu for carrying this treasured lineage across the ocean, and planting it here in San Francisco. The lineage stretches back through time and space to the mists of Wu Tang Mountain, where the legendary Chang San-Feng created Tai-Chi Chuan by applying the principles of ancient Chinese philosophy to the rich tradition of martial arts. The form he created is comprised of sixty-four movements, in correspondence with the sixty-four hexagrams of the *I Ching*, the sourcebook of Chinese philosophy. In every generation the lineage has flourished because there have been dedicated teachers, like Sifu and Simu, who brought the practice alive.

Sifu learned and practiced amid the terrible chaos of China's long and violent revolution. With great courage and skill, he succeeded in carrying the tradition of Tai-Chi Chuan to the West, where it was needed, and where there was sufficient peace and personal liberty for the art to flourish. Simu has created the resources needed for teaching in the modern world—clearly delineating the sixty-four movements, so that Tai-Chi Chuan can be taught and practiced systematically. In her books, Simu has left a valuable pictorial record of the movements, as well as related historical and philosophical material, so that students can study the cultural sources from which the lineage has emerged. Since 1967, many thousands of students have benefited from the teachings of the Lien-Ying Tai-Chi Chuan Academy Sifu and Simu established in San Francisco.

It takes 100 days to decide to learn Tai-Chi Chuan, 1,000 days to learn the movements of the form, and 10,000 days to go beyond the form and bring forth the fruits of the practice.

—Simu Kuo

It is a great blessing to have been given so much time to practice, so that I've actually begun to understand and embody the underlying principles.

My apprenticeship took place at San Francisco State University, where I assisted Simu in teaching her classes for six years. Watching and performing each movement countless times, I carefully imitated Simu's approach in every possible detail. I also paid close attention to how she expressed herself and how she interacted with individual students.

Daily association with Simu was an essential aspect of the apprenticeship: practicing together in the park outside the studio early in the morning, then eating breakfast before driving from Chinatown out to SFSU. I learned a lot about inner aspects of the practice during our drives. Simu talked and I mainly listened, or we were silent. She rarely explains anything verbally, preferring to teach by direct action. Simu does, however, often point to important ideas in parables or stories. A perfect example is her description of how the stages of practice unfold through 10,000 days. Another is what she told me early on about teaching: If you have five dollars in your pocket, only take out and show two. In everything, Simu's approach is to encourage self-reflection and independence. She wants her students to look to themselves, rather than to her, for understanding.

When I first began teaching on my own, I recreated her style as best I could in her absence, scrupulously editing myself out of the situation, sometimes finding her very words and accent on my lips. I never felt entirely satisfied in this role. There was something artificial and therefore mechanical about my approach. I myself didn't feel entirely present. After six long years, though, such was my dedicated habit. Throughout my apprenticeship, Simu had strongly impressed upon me that to change the form is to lose the blessing of the lineage. It was only after several years on my own that I began, out of necessity, to allow what I'd learned to be infused with my own awareness and gifts. My goal has been to preserve the great stature and rigor of the form while being flexible enough to provide students with what they are in a position to receive.

A turning point came for me when I began to teach a class for seniors—a group whose median age was perhaps eighty-five—many with canes and walkers or in wheelchairs, some badly demented. With few exceptions, they could comfortably exercise standing for 15 minutes at most, so I had no choice but to go beyond what I'd learned in my apprenticeship, which had been in the context of physical education for healthy college students. Suddenly I had to be resourceful and creative in my approach, to provide an experience of value for these eager elderly students. In the process, I've used everything from meditation to breathing exercises, self-massage, and prayer.

The situation forced me to inquire into the essence of the art. What would it mean, first of all, to practice Tai-Chi Chuan while seated? I had to find my own way, moment by moment, class by class. The understanding I've come to is that Tai-Chi Chuan is the practice of bringing consciousness to bear upon matter, infusing what is Yin with Yang. Tai-Chi philosophy teaches that everything in this world is part of a single process of continual movement and change. The practical application of the philosophy proceeds by our bringing awareness to the movement of the body, beginning with the breath.

From birth to death, our breathing is a form of continuous movement, but it often becomes restricted due to physical or psychological injuries. A fundamental goal of the practice is the restoration of relaxed and natural breathing, which functions as a rhythmic wave, vitalizing and balancing the different bodily systems, encouraging clarity of feeling, action, and vision. As long as there is consciousness of life, it is possible to practice the essence of Tai-Chi Chuan. Standing, sitting, even lying down—we can always give our attention to breathing, and then allow our other movements to arise and subside in harmony with its rhythm. By *movements*, I mean all our outer movements, whether or not these are the movements of the traditional form. I also mean our inner movements, the modifications of our consciousness, movements of thought and feeling and sensation—the entire range of inner experiences.

Tai-Chi Chuan is taught almost exclusively as a health practice, and it is not generally understood in the West that this practice is rooted in the martial arts, where self-defense and self-cultivation are seen as complementary aspects of a single nameless whole—the *Tao* or "way." On the one hand, the practice of Tai-Chi Chuan is a way of cultivating awareness and sustaining life, by bringing that awareness to bear upon one's body, psyche, and entire existence. In this way, the different faculties (sensation, feeling, thought) are integrated into a shifting whole, and the inner and the outer worlds are attuned, so that one can act with wisdom and compassion. When the body is in a state of inner unity and balance, the breath is relaxed and fluid. Then the mind becomes alert and centered in the heart where the still, small voice of conscience is heard. There is an appreciation for the majestic scale of creation, together with a feeling for what is needed in any given situation. With such inner cohesion and guidance, skillful action can occur effortlessly. In this way, self-defense arises naturally out of the fullness of self-cultivation. One is prey to neither fear nor anger, but is free to respond with flexibility and confidence to the unfolding moment. Of this aspect of the practice, the *I Ching* says, "In the end, the best way to combat evil is to make energetic progress in the good."

153

On the other hand, Tai-Chi Chuan involves diligent practice, which means doing battle with 10,000 shifting adversaries—the entire gamut of inner and outer obstacles and resistance. In self-defense, first of all one must become aware of the tendency to react unconsciously, and in ways that undermine both oneself and others. While the focus of attention must remain grounded in oneself—since it is only from our own root that we can act with real intention and accomplish anything at all—it is important to remember that similar unconscious tendencies are also at play in every single person we encounter!

Self-defense begins by locating and guarding the foundations of consciousness within ourselves, by attending to what's in the body. In this sense, Tai-Chi Chuan training in self-defense is one long exercise in self-purification and patience. One learns to make the right kind of effort by slowly recognizing and discarding all the wrong kinds of effort—what I call "efforting." Driven by unconscious emotional reactivity, such efforting is associated with restriction in breathing, due to the tension required to remain unconscious of how we actually feel. A common example would be trying extra hard to be perfect, out of a deep, unconscious feeling of unworthiness, stemming from deprivation of basic nurturing and love.

The alternative to reacting is waiting and watching and listening and breathing.... In this long, often painful process, we come to know ourselves as we are—with what we really feel—and not as we may imagine ourselves to be. Self-knowledge will arise inevitably in a context of patience and perseverance. An attitude of openness and commitment to ongoing study is necessary for the practice of self-defense to deepen and ripen. Such study embraces oneself and others, indeed every aspect of the world we embody and share. Everything that arises in experience becomes part of the practice—valuable material to be infused with awareness. There is always something important to learn. This is what the tradition calls "continuous self-refinement."

Like the black and white swirls of the Yin-Yang symbol, self-defense and self-cultivation each contains the seed of the other. Integral awareness is the underlying principle of both approaches. When the two are in dynamic balance, the great benefits of Tai-Chi Chuan naturally unfold. When we find the patience to contain our emotional reactivity and reclaim our projections, we begin to make peace within ourselves, bringing fragmented aspects of the whole back into relationship. This is what Bodhidharma has called "extinguishing all outflows." Conceived as it is in loving awareness, inner peace naturally gives rise to the wish, and then the capacity, to cooperate in making peace in the world.

The key has been learning to listen to what's in my body: following sensation into feeling and insight, rather than into the battery of emotional reactivity.

—J. K.

I would also like to share something of my experience during the twelve years since my apprenticeship at SFSU ended. My goal here is to offer an authentic, personal perspective on the idea that it takes 10,000 days to go beyond the form and begin to bring forth the fruits of the practice. This has been a time for learning to apply the principles of Tai-Chi philosophy not only in my teaching, but also to my situation in life.

From this perspective, the 10,000 days of practice correspond to the 10,000 defeats out of which the true person fashions a single victory. Like most people, I tend to imagine that I want things to be easy. I want to feel that I am succeeding, winning. I want to feel that I am in control. In reality, though, much of my growth has come out of the struggle to embrace my many shortcomings, inner obstacles, and broken places. Without some such struggle, I doubt that it is possible to bring forth the abundant fruits of Tai-Chi Chuan practice.

Not long before the end of my apprenticeship with Simu in 1990, my mother died after a long illness, during which I was one of her two primary caregivers. At the same time, a decade of quasi-monastic celibacy gave way to involvement in a close relationship, really for the first time in my life. I was soon in emotional upheaval, and within a few months I became terribly sick with pulmonary influenza. The illness disrupted my twice-daily practice, and before I knew it I was spiraling into a massive depression. Feelings of grief and helplessness, rage and despair suddenly surfaced with ferocious intensity. Severely stricken in the lungs for several months, I was so sick I couldn't even get near the golden glow I'd long been getting out my practice. Without a way out, I had to begin to find a way into my painful feelings.

Since the physical symptoms centered in my lungs, I decided to try holotropic breath therapy, in which continuous deep breathing is used to open and explore the uncharted psycho-spiritual holdings (samsaras) of one's inner world. Within minutes of my first session, I was on my back screaming, "Get off of me, get off of me…." Along with the screaming arose the unsettling certainty that I was caught in the re-enactment of some early childhood trauma. I had no conscious awareness of the situation to which my suffering was connected, but the sensations and feelings themselves were unmistakable. Only after I'd learned to listen to myself in quite a new way would I come to a clearer understanding of what my body was telling me….

So, during the past twelve years, as I've been slowly learning to teach Tai-Chi Chuan, I've also been engaged in a sometimes desperate search for my own healing. It was clear that I had been using intensive practice as a kind of "spiritual bypass" to stay pumped up above lifelong psycho-physical wounding. I was both horrified and fascinated to see what surfaced when my practice crashed: the same horrible feelings and issues I'd been struggling with when initially I connected with Simu as a floundering adolescent and began to practice Tai-Chi Chuan and meditation in earnest. These were also the feelings that had tormented me since before I could remember, the feelings I'd done my best to suppress in childhood by throwing myself into "being good"—excelling in my studies and becoming something of a compulsive caregiver in my family and later in school.

Though I continued to teach and practice Tai-Chi Chuan and meditation regularly, for many years I felt really shattered. During this time I was fortunate to connect with an excellent psychotherapist, someone who'd originally trained in bodywork and who embraced a non-dogmatic spiritual perspective, so that self-inquiry and holistic healing were possible in his presence. Also key here were the few relationships in which I was able to communicate about what I was slowly discovering about my childhood. These were relationships with people unafraid of intensely painful feelings, generally because they themselves were (or had been) engaged in similar processes of self-remembering. Other important resources for my journey into memory and feeling have been daily writing and prayer. Writing is something I'd already been doing for many years. It was simply a question of using it for psycho-physical self-inquiry. Prayer has emerged only as I've begun to listen to my inner voice and embrace what I feel and need.

Unlocking the repression of early childhood memory has meant uncovering powerful defensive reactivity and slowly learning to live with the disturbing feelings long hidden underneath. Living in a state of feeling has been almost entirely new to me. Indeed, one reason I initially took refuge in Tai-Chi Chuan and meditation practice with such intensity was to avoid the emotional distress that had plagued me throughout my life. The key has been learning to listen to what's in my body: following sensation into feeling and insight, rather than into the defensive battery of emotional reactivity and fragmentation. This means moving into an acceptance of need rather than avoiding it, as I was trained to do early in life.

I have approached the process with the same persistence and determination with which I embrace Tai-Chi Chuan itself. Along with much pain, there have been many rewards, not the least being that my practice no longer serves as a "spiritual bypass." Instead I am able to bring a much deeper quality of presence and concentration to the challenges and opportunities I encounter.

As always, I have sought to apply the basic principles of Tai-Chi philosophy to this new kind of work. In the context of self-remembering, applying the principles means intentionally directing consciousness (which is Yang) into the body (which is Yin), and allowing what arises to unfold without interfering. I've had to learn to pay attention, accept and go into painful feelings—rather than avoid them via compulsive practice, numbing, or just plain distraction. Timing is crucial in this process: learning to pace myself, so I don't get overwhelmed and lost in pain. Pacing myself has also meant learning to create sanctuary and safety around myself, so that I can rest and gather force for more work. Here too, I've found my way only slowly, discovering what works by discarding what doesn't. What's needed is the patience to weigh whatever arises in the light of conscience, to contain and take responsibility for the projects of emotional reactivity, to wait in trust for openness and love to flower in the heart.

My relationship with Simu has provided an unexpected and important arena for my healing, because it has given me an opportunity to rework the defensive caregiving pattern with which I was programmed early in life. Simu has the instincts of a great Tai-Chi master. She understands the importance of both self-defense and self-cultivation. She cares about her students and senses what they need for their development.

In the years since my apprenticeship, Simu has continued to push with infallible precision—not too hard, not too soft—on the very places of my deepest defensiveness and wounding. It's only in recent years, as I've become more present and whole, that I've finally pushed back in earnest and found my autonomy and inner authority. So Simu has taught me self-defense through the dynamics of our relationship, forcing me gently, in a process like "pushing-hands," to find my ground. I've slowly learned how to push back and "repulse the monkey" of reactive mind with an open heart. As in pushing-hands, the challenge has been to remain alert and responsive, to embrace the moment and move like a tiger finding its way in the mountains.

This is why I consider self-remembering and recovery of the
inner world … an essential aspect of self-defense.

—J. K.

Self-remembering is really a form of soul retrieval. It means recovering the whole of one's inner world. This is the world most of us are compelled, in one way or another, to forsake in early childhood, the world of our own deepest feelings and essence. What we recover in the process of self-remembering often includes experiences of great joy and great suffering from the very beginnings of life. Such memories were recorded when we still were in a state of complete dependency, before we could use words to organize experience. They emerge not as visual memories with clear narrative and context, but as a confusing and intense jumble of fragments—sensations, feelings, and (later) thoughts—often distorted by great fear and other forms of defensive reactivity. This is the cloud of confusion we must eventually see through and dispel to achieve concentration.

Repression of early childhood memories is such a universal phenomenon that we tend not to see how strange it is, being unable to remember anything that happened when we were very young. In every culture I'm aware of—certainly in all of the "dominant" cultures—a major goal of child-rearing and educational practices is repression of the intense and unwieldy feelings of early childhood. Such repression is generally accomplished through shaming and contempt for what is fearful and needy, for the actual feelings of the child. One result is a society in which the great majority of the population is in more or less complete amnesia about the most formative experiences of their lives.

So long we remain embedded in a cohesive family and culture, where there is a clear sense of stability and shared values, perhaps it is possible to thrive without having much access to the inner world of our own feelings. In the modern world, though, with the rise of technology and globalization in so many forms, conditions of social upheaval and culture clash are increasingly prevalent. Without the rudder of our own feelings and sense of value, it is extremely difficult to find direction and meaning in such circumstances. Instead we remain caught in our own internalized defensiveness, the patterns of which were laid down in the first months and years of life. In such a posture of unconscious victimization, we easily fall prey to manipulation by fear-based, power-seeking people, organizations, ideologies, and mass movements. This is why I consider self-remembering and recovery of the inner world not only a matter of self-cultivation, but also an essential aspect of self-defense.

Although the particular details of my story are of course unique, the basic scenario is more or less universal. As Simu might say, in this whole world, there's only one body and one soul. I was born in the shadow of war, into a family and a culture based on the repression of feeling and suppression of the awareness of the inner world. By the time I left home, I was hungry for meaning and love, without really understanding why. I was also completely unconscious of the extensive psycho-physical injuries I had sustained and now embodied. I imagined I was completely free, and I had no idea that my injuries would inevitably limit and shape my possibilities in life. I was quite unaware of my vulnerability, and without any access to my own feelings, soon began to flounder for lack of direction, and fall prey....

I am extremely grateful to have encountered Simu and become her student, since in a very real sense, I would say that Tai-Chi Chuan has saved my life. It gave me the means to reconnect with the wellsprings of my being, and has been an invaluable resource at every stage of my ongoing healing and individuation. Like most spiritual traditions, however, Tai-Chi Chuan was created—and its methods of transmission and practice established—before the truly revolutionary discoveries of modern psychology. Therefore some of its methods need to be revised in accordance with what we now know. Early childhood experience lays down patterns that stay with us throughout our lives. When such patterns involve basic self-suppression, as they almost always do, they can make us confused and vulnerable, unable to flourish. It is important that teaching and practice occur in an atmosphere free of coercion, shaming, and excessive competition—however subtle—since these are the standard methods for compelling young children to suppress themselves. Otherwise, our efforts easily become covert means of perpetuating the misery of living by force and in fear. True inner peace will not arise in such an atmosphere, especially not with the conditions prevalent in the modern world.

When students of Tai-Chi Chuan (or other disciplines) encounter difficulties in concentration and in deepening their practice, the traditional "advice" has been to try harder, to think positively, and not to give energy to nagging negative feelings. Certainly there is much to be said for simply trying and remaining underway. A problem arises, however, when such advice encourages the unconscious and erroneous assumption that it is impossible to decipher the bodymind's coded language of signs and symptoms. Within this misconception lurks the belief that it is not possible to remember, understand, and integrate the facts about one's early past into present time awareness. Much that is destructive in religious dogma and spiritual practice can be traced to this misconception—and its usual corollary: There's no point in trying to make sense of all that. Better to forget it and move on. Project oneself into the mind's heaven … which eventually metamorphoses into the hell we've been striving to avoid.

The tradition of Tai-Chi Chuan is truly fortunate in that it sticks to the basic principles of interweaving Yin and Yang, and is more or less without dogma. The tradition will certainly grow and continue to flourish to the extent that it succeeds in incorporating the discoveries of modern science into its methods. As I've tried to illustrate with my own story, our past persists in the present like the rings in a tree. This is one of the central findings of modern psychology, that we embody and carry the patterns with which we are imprinted early in life, right down to the cellular, hormonal, and neurological levels. But this discovery runs counter to the traditional belief that phenomena such as memory and feeling and thought are more or less immaterial abstractions, which an individual can control or even banish at will.

In the practice and teaching of Tai-Chi Chuan, it is essential that we clear away misconceptions as they arise, so that we may continue to incorporate new understandings. In this way, we become increasingly present and able to apply the principles of Tai-Chi philosophy—infusing what we embody with loving awareness. My own experience has been that freedom in the inner world is not at all a given. On the contrary, it arises only out of long, hard work—which includes both self-cultivation and self-defense. The work of continuous self-refinement was going on before we were born, it will continue after we are gone. We are all of us in this together—that is the teaching. Despite myriad setbacks and minor defeats, we do gradually make progress in the good.

Jeffrey Kessler, Simu Kuo, John Bratten,
Jonas Hamilton

Choosing Tai-Chi Chuan

RICHARD PRAEGER

*Richard Praeger, at age seventy-two, practices
Movement 2, Grasp Bird's Tail.*

In April 1994, a friend of mine from Sacramento, who, like I, was retired, loaned me *Tai Chi for Health* by Edward Maisel, urging me to read it and to inquire about teachers in the Bay Area.

Jack has long been a health activist in exercise and diet. Since 1976 he has been practicing the "Yang long form," with its 108 movements, every day. I had a heart attack in March, and he was convinced that it would be an ideal exercise form for me.

A former skier and jogger, I had stopped after orthoscopic knee surgery and had no special exercise at that time.

I called and visited Simmone Kuo and we discussed her approach. I quickly decided to work with her, and my first lesson was in October 1994. At the start I felt I was not doing as well as I should, but that I was learning something new every week with a lesson on Friday and a review on Sunday. The important thing was that I really wanted to learn, and I recognized that Simmone was an exceptional teacher.

I practice every day for about a half-hour. In the beginning it consisted of many repetitions of the movements learned to date. In 1995, before a spring trip to Paris, I realized that I was nearing completion of the sixty-four movements and that I could learn the balance on my return. I worked on memorizing the names of the movements while doing them, and developing a consistency in timing. Having completed the sixty-four steps with Simmone's help, my practices grew to consist of two repetitions of the full set.

On my return to San Francisco in September 1995, Simmone concentrated much more on form. It was only then that I realized that her preliminary teaching method for beginners de-emphasized form in favor of the substance of the steps until the student is familiar with the essence and order of the sixty-four movements. This had been most helpful to me, though I'd been unaware of it at the time. I tend to be impatient with myself during any learning process, and having attention called to my errors while learning the full set would have hindered my progress. Now, as I receive corrections on form, I accept them as a necessary step in gaining personal satisfaction from Tai-Chi Chuan.

One of the most important benefits of the exercises for me is the knowledge that they require complete concentration to do them correctly. If I let my mind wander toward personal problems, I am certain to make errors. On the other hand, I can take some interruptions from others, which happens fairly frequently at Crissy Field, my San Francisco site, and return to the interrupted movement, continuing without error as long as I don't start mulling over either the interruption or some personal problem. Thus the exercises have become a most important relief or perhaps even escape from useless worries.

Another important advantage has been an improvement in balance. Though I hadn't expected many problems in this area because of more than twenty years of skiing, I now realize that the speed in that sport is a natural aid to overcoming balance problems. I experienced difficulties with balance while learning Golden Cock Stands on One Leg, but after working at it many times I've managed to do it fairly well, even in strong cross or tail winds. It is now my favorite movement, and I constantly try to improve it.

I remain disappointed in my performance of leg kick movements such as Separation of Right (and Left) Foot, Left Leg Kicks Up, Forward, and Turn and Kick with Sole. I thought at first that it might have to do with my polio problems, but as my paralysis only limits my right leg and hip, that seems like a poor excuse, especially since I don't recognize a similar problem with Cross Wave of Water Lily nor Wave Lotus Foot, both right leg kicks.

I certainly attribute a large measure of importance to Tai-Chi Chuan for my present general feeling of health, well-being, and enthusiasm.

Experience of Philosophy

Mark Nelson

Tai-Chi Chuan is one of the internal martial arts, as opposed to the external arts such as kung-fu or karate. In the internal arts, it is the mind that is the prime mover.

The word *tai-chi* is seen as the union of the primal forces Yang and Yin, positive and negative, light and dark. The conception of Tai-Chi as the union of Yang and Yin can be seen in the basic advice given to students of the Tai-Chi Chuan art. One's movements are to be "not too slow, not too fast; not too hard, not too soft." In short, the movements of Tai-Chi Chuan are to be balanced.

In the ancient Tai-Chi philosophy, which later informed the development of the martial art, keen attention was paid to the connections and balance between all things. Nothing could be all light, or all dark, all hard or all soft. The ancient Tai-Chi philosophy focused also on an analysis of the properties of things through the five elements and the eight trigrams of the *I Ching*.

The eight trigrams of the *I Ching* represent the eight possible configurations of the Yin and Yang, when they are taken three at a time. (The first trigram has three solid lines to denote three Yang, the second has a broken line, then two solid lines to denote one Yin followed by two Yang, and so on.) If these trigrams are combined to form hexagrams, there are sixty-four possible combinations of Yin and Yang. These sixty-four combinations were thought to express all the possible states of change in the universe. This belief informed the later development of the Tai-Chi Chuan art, as there are exactly sixty-four movements in the form.

Something I find interesting in the philosophy of the art is expressed in Master Kuo's mnemonic of the Thirteen Movements:

> All changes and motions are conceived and touched off in the
>   stillness of absolute quietude,
> Hence motion and action are kindred to rest and inaction,
> in other words, ultimately indistinguishable from each other.
>   —Kuo Lien-Ying

This quote captures something that—though made much of in recent years by Western philosophers seeking to relate to Eastern philosophy—is still underappreciated. To say that motion and action are indistinguishable from each other is equivalent to the notion in modern physics that absolute motion and absolute rest are indistinguishable, that they are qualities that are relative to the state of the observer—much as the mnemonic goes on to say, "It is your opponent's movements that condition your own...."It is remarkable that this idea could be developed through an appreciation for the movements of the body and their symmetry with the motions of an opponent, while the complementary idea in the West required the abstraction of a mathematical approach to motion.

This kind of analogy between the body and mathematics is in part what drove me to study Tai-Chi in the first place. My intellectual interests are in the relationships among different fields of study, and the way that similar ideas can be explored using a wide variety of methods within different fields. For example, the concept of unity is treated intellectually in the Western philosophical tradition, symbolically in mathematics, and metaphorically through literature, dance, and Tai-Chi with its accompanying philosophy.

Another interest in Tai-Chi lies in its insistence on balance in movement and thought. This kind of balance is something frequently missing in the Western tradition, which tends to overemphasize either body or mind at the expense of the other. This balance has been a great personal aid to me, first as I began Tai-Chi while recovering from knee surgery, and in recent months as a way to relax and focus at a time when world affairs and collective insanity seemed to impinge on everything I did.

Confucius

Lecture given by Zhao Demei at Qufu, China (Birthplace of Confucius) on May 22, 2001, based on the *In the Mansion of Confucius' Descendents* text by Kong de Mo.

> A sense of the contrasts of life brings the awareness of being
>   alive.
> What you say no to in life cannot enter your experience.
> *Chant the beauty of the good and stop barking against the bad.*
> —EMERSON

There are quite a few Confucian terms that do not translate directly from Chinese into English. In China, "thought" is bigger than "concept," which is too concrete. "Judgment" is a conclusion or decision; "image" is the inner meaning; and mistake involves no blame, because you can correct any error. "Remorse" does not exist for Confucians, because the law of your mind holds no grudge against you. The past is forgotten/remembered no more.

Confucius lived 551–479 B.C.E., the Spring and Autumn Periods of the Zhou Dynasty, a time when there were many philosophers. During the Zhou Dynasty, there was complete disorder, and the emperor faced poverty. A sparsified political and economic situation led to an awareness of the necessity of the people's support, which could be achieved by giving more support to the people.

This could only come through ideological change, in which the focus of the government was switched from Heaven to the people and was enriched, developed, and systematized. The character for benevolence appeared a little before Confucius' time, and the concept was integrated into the political context of his day.

This provided for an environment for learning in which the political atmosphere was initially conducive to the development of Confucian ideology. Confucian ideas were accepted as the official ideology in 146 B.C.E. during the Han Dynasty, three hundred years after Confucius' death. His descendents studied what he wrote down as textbooks. Unfortunately, Ching Tse Huong burned Confucius' books during the Qin Dynasty (221–207 B.C.E.) because he wanted *power*. Although recognition of Confucian ideas came and went over the centuries, his life and works have commanded great respect.

Confucius' position in feudal society was prominent. The year after his death, his house was turned into Confucius Temple. His books, robes, and musical instruments are stored here. In 194 B.C.E., the first Emperor of the Han Dynasty came to Qufu to worship Confucius (state ideology established/ offered sacrifices). This custom remained until the end of the Qing Dynasty (1644–1911). In other words, it lasted through the entire period of feudal society. This royal offering became state custom.

In C.E. 1 Confucius was canonized as Marquis of Illustrious Praise, "Duke Nyin." In C.E. 630, Confucian Temples were built throughout the country, and official worship began. In 860, pictures of Confucius were introduced to all classrooms as ideal teacher, and the custom of bowing to the teacher as the student entered was put into place. In 1723, five generations of Confucius' ancestors were canonized as Kings/Princes, and were honored as first (#1) family in Heaven.

Confucius' family lived in the Hunan Province (Sang State), and he was born at the foot of Mt. Ni as Zhongni Qiu. His name *Kong Fuzi* means "Master Kong" = Confucius. He was a creator and preserver of Chinese history and all that is good in Chinese culture. Confucius absorbed the good elements of Taoism and Buddhism. The Nucleus/Premise/Quintessence of Confucian philosophy is *Benevolence*, as a foundation for political, ethical, and educational ideas.

The most important implication of the idea of Benevolence for Chinese political rulers was to love the people. One famous philosophy goes something like this: "Those who are to rule a large state of 1,000 chariots … [shall] practice economy in expenditure and love for the people." When governing is by punishment (*law*), there is no sense of right and wrong; but when governing is by example (*virtue*), a sense of right and wrong is instilled. Within this context, the people have control over themselves, which instills a sense of *propriety*. This leads to cooperation, which makes the people easy to govern, maintains good social order, and leads individuals to self-cultivation.

Benevolence

Confucius in court costume

Philosophical Background: The Teachings of Confucius as Related to Tai-Chi and Tai-Chi Chuan

Shannon Cook

Aiding in the teaching of Tai-Chi Chuan has been a rewarding experience in many aspects. Not only is it enriching for my teaching experience and enlightening to my own learning process, but it also provides a space for me to explore the philosophy behind the movements of Tai-Chi Chuan. The investigation of Tai-Chi principles involves the investigation of a way of life based on Confucian standards of conduct learned by every Chinese young person in school. These fundamental teachings correspond to the goals of Tai-Chi. This is called *ch'eng jen*, or becoming a complete person who has knowledge, freedom from covetousness, bravery, talent, propriety, righteousness, and rhythm.

The accomplishment of these goals in Tai-Chi Chuan is neither immediate nor obvious. Knowledge comes from persistent practice through which one comes to know the body and its temporal limits. Freedom from covetousness comes from the sense of unattachment that one can achieve through quiet daily practice. A realization of what is truly important can follow through this opportunity for introspection. Bravery comes with the self-confidence and talent developed through regular physical exercise. Propriety, or *li*, is an inner sense of morality that can be developed through sensing the true nature of the self and through regulating harmony. This also involves not extending one's energy before one is sure that the result will be beneficial to both parties involved—the concept of reciprocity, or *jen*. The righteousness, or *yi*, that arises from integrating *yi, jen, li,* and *te* (virtue) are imbued in the rhythm of the Tai-Chi form and the regularity its practice can give to one's life.

The concept of *te* is greatly discussed by the Chinese philosopher Confucius (sixth century B.C.E.) and is documented by his students such as Mencius. *Te* means virtue, integrity, nature, and the ability of something or someone to follow its own nature. Tai-Chi Chuan's form allows the body to relax to such an extent that it becomes aware and in tune with its own nature, *te*, and also with nature around it. This furthers one along the path, or *tao*. Following nature creates harmony and an awareness of harmony.

As a student of Tai-Chi, I have been led to the path of self-examination and searching for true virtue and my own true nature (*te*). Many of the teachings of Confucius are reflected in learning and practicing Tai-Chi Chuan. Faithfulness and sincerity are principles through which one should not fear to mend one's way when one makes a mistake. Through avoiding frustration, one can speed progress. Consistency and doing one's best in action, seeking to perfect admirable qualities in the self and to encourage them in others, and leading by example are all patterns not easily developed; yet they are gently encouraged by the experienced teacher and heeded by the diligent student of Tai-Chi Chuan and Tai-Chi philosophy.

In the Confucian *Analects*, the ancient philosopher Confucius says that a leader in society should work to do the following: Exalt virtue by doing what is to be done, with success as a secondary consideration; reform the depraved by assailing one's own weakness, not that of others; and discover misguided judgment by not giving way to small things nor having fits of anger. The concept of *jen*, or benevolence, works hand in hand with the more complex belief of *chung kung*, which means, "Do not unto others as you would not want them to do unto you." There is no room for self-deception in the search for true excellence and true sincerity.

Thus virtue (*te*) is extremely important in Confucian philosophy, not only for the leader, but also for the student, who holds a special place of respect in society. Virtue is firm, enduring, simple, modest, and earnest. Modesty is inherent, and the good student decides cautiously and investigates all things to the extreme. This enriches the learner, who devotes his or her spare energy to cultivating a greater capacity for learning. The wise embrace all knowledge, but are most earnest about what is of greater importance. The three most important questions to ask oneself as a good student are (1) Have I done my best? (2) Have I been sincere and trustworthy with friends? and (3) Have I mastered and practiced the instructions of my teacher?

In keeping with these concepts, we can see that the applied practice of Tai-Chi Chuan and the assiduous study of Tai-Chi philosophy lead to fulfillment through undisturbed self-activity. These studies provide an opportunity for extensive self-reflection and self-realization through coming closer to what is natural for the body and the mind. The intrinsic integrity involved in learning, or *hsueh*, involves *jen*, or reciprocity, and benevolence in not deviating from one's own nature in providing what another needs. Mutual benefit is evident in the relationships of parent–child, husband–wife, older brother–younger brother, ruler–subject, friend–friend, and teacher–student. The sincerity that exists between the two parties creates culture, or *wen*—a beautiful pattern or the beautiful qualities the student has acquired through education. This beautiful pattern is reflected in the Tai-Chi form and in the feeling of peace and love of life that result from attentive practice. The harmony experienced within reflects in life relationships and in an underlying yet all-pervading hint of bliss. Eternal vigilance of this harmony in blending and balancing Yin and Yang (knowledge and practice) in life brings us closer to the "ultimate or absolute point" of the self, or *Tai-Chi*.

The ethics of Confucianism are based on the following theories:

> 1. The Universe is regulated by an Order that is moral in its essence.
>
> 2. Man is morally good by nature, and it rests with him to remain so.
>
> 3. Man errs from ignorance and the force of bad example.
>
> 4. The remedies are education of the official classes and good example set by them.
>
> 5. The individual must rectify himself before he can rectify others. He must study the teachings of the Ancients and be well versed in the modern ritualistic rules and social observances.
>
> 6. Above all it is essential to cultivate the Five Virtues: benevolence, justice, propriety, wisdom, sincerity.

It is to be noted that Confucius also has a place assigned to him among the deities of the Taoist religion, and he is addressed as honored one of Heaven who causes literature to flourish and the world to prosper.

Tai-Chi and *I*

DAN Y.P. WANG

Several years of research have gone into studying a problem that has been on my mind for some time now. Because of various circumstances in my life, I could not ignore the problem. Technological developments, such as the advancements in space travel and computer technology, have also changed my personal life. I've had to throw away all that I had previously established in my professional life, and start from scratch: a new lonely journey. At that time, computer technology was only a tiny light at the end of the tunnel; the road through the tunnel was long, dark, and lonely, but the tiny light was getting bigger and brighter. I taught computer science at the university for more than three years. I worked for Amdahl Corporation for more than seven years, and I excelled in trouble-shooting complex mainframe computers. I enjoyed challenging and rebalancing my life. These are all typical examples of how technological development can affect how our society and culture change. It is a part of the constant change of almost everything on Earth and beyond, and of an ongoing process of control, creation, and matching. In one phase, *I* is the key to the relationship between technology and social or cultural change.

Both in America and Europe, Yin-Yang or Tai-Chi is frequently encountered and widely accepted, especially at the college and university level. Most people know something about Tai-Chi. However, when asked the questions "Why?"; "What is the origin?"; "How is the whole system organized?"; "When and how was it connected to modern technological development?"; or "What are the truly ongoing meanings?" the right answers are seldom, if ever, heard. Having spent many hours and many days searching for the true answers, I would like to share my findings.

The word *I* ("Change") has given its name to the book known as the *I Ching*. The two characters, *I* and *Ching*, have very interesting original meanings. The origin of the Chinese character *I* is the form of a lizard, which, in the wilderness, constantly and naturally changes the color of its body according to the time of the day or its environment. Therefore, *I* means, logically and literally, "changing forever" or "easily, naturally" like the lizard. The second character *Ching* means "constants," "rules," or "unchangeables." One of the important principles of the *I Ching* is that if we can understand and apply the rules, the unchangeables, then we can master the forever-changing complex easily and naturally, technological development and our forever-changing nature.

I in *I Ching*

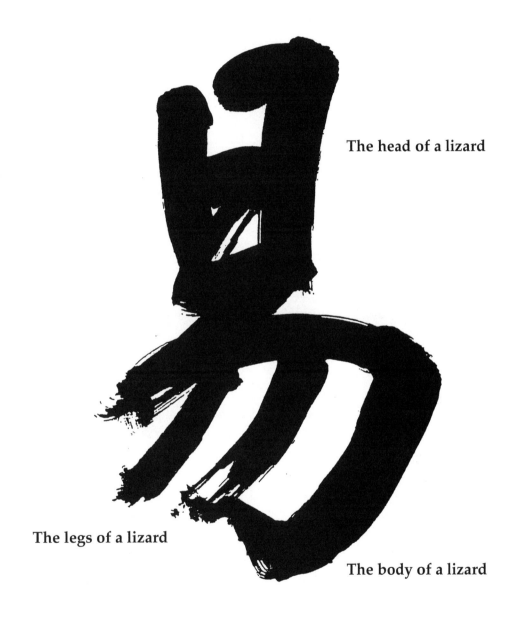

The head of a lizard

The legs of a lizard

The body of a lizard

Looking at the pictorial Chinese word *I* (易), one can see that it has a round head, a twisting and winding body, and a number of legs. The origin of the Chinese character *I* is the form of a lizard, which moves easily from one place to another, changing the color of its body. Furthermore, the lizard can regenerate its tail in time.

For at least three thousand years, but no doubt longer, the *I Ching* has been used as a book of divination (the process that seeks to foresee or to foretell future events). It is probably the oldest book in the world and is the very origin of the Yin-Yang or Tai-Chi system.

Can we label the *I Ching* as simply superstition? Studies reveal that the Tai-Chi system of the *I Ching* is not only a well-balanced, unique logic system based on Yin-Yang (Relativity), but also a scientifically organized philosophical system based on the principles of higher mathematics and quantum physics. The whole system was structured from Wu-Chi to Yin/Yang to Tai-Chi to eight trigrams and finally to sixty-four hexagrams.

The circle that represents the whole is divided into Yin (black) and Yang (white)—two polar complements in harmonious balance that describe how things function in relation to each other and beyond. The smaller circles (the eyes), shaded in the opposite color, illustrate that within Yin there is Yang, and vice versa, and explain the continuous process of balanced change. The dynamic curve dividing them indicates that Yin and Yang are continuously merging in a give-and-take relationship. Thus Yin and Yang create each other, control each other, and transform into each other in two types of transformations: changes that occur harmoniously in the normal course of events, and the sudden ruptures and transformations associated with extremely disharmonious situations. Because Yin and Yang create each other in even the most stable relationship, Yin and Yang are always subtly transforming into each other. This constant transformation is the source of all change—in a dynamic manner. There are no absolutes; no entity can ever be isolated from its relationship to other entities; no thing can exist in and of itself. Yin and Yang must, necessarily, contain within themselves the possibility of opposition and change.

In a relationship where Yin and Yang are unbalanced for prolonged periods of time, or in an extreme manner, the resulting transformations may be quite drastic. Harmony means that the proportions of Yin and Yang are relatively balanced; disharmony means that the proportions are unequal and there is imbalance. A deficiency of one aspect implies an excess of the other. Extreme disharmony means that the deficiency of one aspect cannot continue to support the excess of the other aspect. The resulting change may be rebalancing, or, if that is not possible, either the transformation into opposites or the cessation of existence. Good examples are the greenhouse effect and the Yi-Ho Garden of the Summer Palace built by Empress Dowager Tsi Hsi at the end of the Ching Dynasty. The greenhouse effect results from the neglect of the Earth, with the effects of nuclear power, the Cold War of the 1980s, and the resulting hole in the ozone layer, which is currently affecting the weather and ecosystems of the world.

The hexagrams (six-line structures) are made up of two types of lines: solid lines being Yang and broken lines being Yin. The sixty-four hexagrams display every possible combination of these, taken six lines at a time, resulting in $2^6 = 64$.

To define *I* more clearly, let's look at an example: We cannot overemphasize the importance of the development of human energy (four lower energy centers) and earth energy (such as geothermal and tidal resources) that barely touch each other. There are many examples of imbalance within these, where adjustments are long due.

Things in the technological field are always in a state of flux and change; and these changes, though endless, progress from the easy and simple to the difficult and complex. In other words, things in this field are complex and forever changing, but if we follow the order for change, then among the complexities, simplicity can be found, and among the changes, something unchanging. Because of this, the *I* is that by which the scholars searched the depths—to explore what is complex, to prove what is hidden, to bring to the surface what lies deep, to reach what is distant—and investigated the hidden springs, examined the slight beginnings of movement and the earliest indications of events. Only through the depths could they penetrate and view everything in the fields. Only through the hidden springs could they complete all of the undertakings in the fields.

The relationship between technological development and social or cultural change is somewhat like the relationship of Yin/Yang. They create each other, control each other, and balance each other. Otherwise, the price to pay for rebalancing can be very great.

The Chi and Tao of *I Ching*

DAN Y. P. WANG

There are numerous questions which are fascinating in regards to Chi and Tao of *I Ching*. What is the Complementary principle and the theory of Relativity? How can we learn about the Tao of *I Ching*? When and how did the European people learn about the Tao of *I Ching*? What have the European scholars learned from the Hexagram table? Who, when, and for what purpose was the first Binary system of the world designed?

In recent years, because of the rapid development of high-tech computers and transportation, the world we live in, in a sense, is shrinking rapidly. People have more and more opportunity to travel and to meet each other. The conflicts of multinational, diverse cultures are also quickly escalating. This provides a background for harmonious relations between the peoples of the world and between those people and their environment.

Throughout history, leaders and scholars have sought better ways not only to harmonize relationships among all kinds of people, but also to integrate interdependencies with Mother Nature in order to have better living, improved health, and lengthened life span. In other words, they have looked for ways to create a better civilization and to create a holistic environment for people to live in.

In this regard, abstracting from classroom practice, one of the best knowledge systems, which has been proven by modern science and great scholars worldwide, is the Tao of *I Ching*. The origin of this system is the Eight Diagrams invented by Fu Hsi (2953–2852 B.C.E..). He was the first of the earliest Three Emperors of the legendary period of China. Fu Hsi wisely used two simple characters, - - (the broken line) and — (the solid line), to represent not only the constant, perpetual Yin and Yang patterns, but also the dynamic, ongoing complementary relationships of them, which include primal polarities on many levels: zero-one, odd-even, day-night, light-dark, male-female, hot-cold, long-short, bitter-sweet, positive-negative, and so forth. The most important point is that it controls everything that is happening in the whole universe including human cell reproduction (which will be explicated later …).

Looking at the pictorial Chinese word *I* (易), one can see that it has a round head, a twisting and winding body, and a number of legs. According to Chinese etymological dictionary, the character "I" (易) originates from the picture of "lizard." Observed in the wilderness, the lizard moves easily from one place to another, and changes its color from one situation to the next. Furthermore, the lizard cannot only easily cut off its tail from the body whenever necessary, but it can also recreate its tail again in time. Because of the changeability of the lizard, the word "I" was adopted for *I Ching*.

The Tao of *I Ching* describes this changing process, based on the detachment and attachment of the separation and union of lines. The separation line is one-in-two (Yin, - -) which always changes to two-in-one (Yang, —). Yang is division brought together in union, and changes into Yin. That is the duality—the dynamic, ceaseless, and interdependent nature of the relational symbols of the Yin and Yang forces. The primary function of Yin and Yang is none other than to provide for and illustrate the relationship of universal counterparts. These counterparts are not actually separate but form a universal whole, which can be represented by the eight trigrams.

The Eight Trigram system is rooted in Oneness. In the process of transformation, it propagated Yin (- -) and Yang (—) as two poles. From Yin and Yang were generated four forces (Strong Yin, Weakening Yin, Weak Yang, and Strong Yang, and so on). Finally, these developed into Eight Trigrams. In other words: One propagates the two Poles (Yin and Yang); in the process of transformation, they generate the four forces. Consequently, the Eight Trigrams were developed.

The following table illustrates the Eight Diagrams' structural evolution.

Tai-Chi (Grand Ultimate)

Yin Pole (Strong Yin) Yang Pole (Strong Yang)

Tai Yin / Strong Yin	Shao Yang / Weak Yang	Shao Yin / Weak Yin	Tai Yang / Strong Yang

TRIGRAM

ELEMENT

Earth Kuen	Mountain Genn	Water Kann	Wind Shiun	Thunder Jenn	Fire Li	Lake Duey	Heaven Chyan

This system was not only a closely guarded secret which was passed on from one Master to selected students, but was also never imagined to eventually be taught to Westerners (all people belonging to European civilization).

During the seventeenth century, one of the Jesuit missionaries in China, Father Joachim Bouvet, went back to Europe, and showed the Hexagram table of the *I Ching* and the entire system to Gottfried Wilhelm Leibniz, a well-known German philosopher and mathematician. Leibniz was amazed and moved. The unbelievable coincidence of Leibniz's binary system of seventeenth century and the Hexagram of *I Ching* table, in about 2865 years B.C.E., has become a real point of interest for the history of science.

The interaction of Yin and Yang presupposed their offspring, the creative process. Therefore, in a later period, it became important in the development of organic naturalism by many scholars like Chuang Chou, Chou Tun-I, Chu His, and so forth. The Western leading scholar of Eastern thought, Joseph Needham, the Director of Cambridge University of London, England, also summed up the importance of the Chinese philosophical view of the Yin and Yang system to the development of contemporary science as the following:

The time was to come when the growth of knowledge necessitated the adoption of a more organic philosophy no less naturalistic than atomic materialism. That was the time of Darwin, Frazer, Pasteur, Freud, Spemann, Planck, and Einstein. When it came, a line of philosophical thinkers was found to have prepared the way—from Whitehead back to Engels and Hegel, from Hegel to Leibniz—then perhaps the inspiration was not European at all. Perhaps the theoretical foundations of the most modern European's natural science owe more to the men such as Chuang Chou, Chou Tou-I, and Chu His than the world has yet realized.

The most intriguing and interesting point was that, within these Yin and Yang patterns, if we substitute the solid-line for zero and the broken-line for one, the Eight Diagram system is nothing else but the first, perfect binary system of the world which is arranged according to the natural processes of development recognized and documented by Fu Hsi. Fu Hsi wisely used two simple characters, the broken line and the solid line to represent not only the Yin and Yang, respectively, but also their dynamic complementary relationships, which include primal polarities on many levels. Moreover, the Eight Diagram system was a Yin and Yang two-value system, just like "ON" and "OFF" circuitry. The Yin (- -) assembled the open circuit (or "OFF" position), because the middle of the line was open (the broken line). The Yang (—) assembled the closed circuit (or "ON" position), because its center was closed, a solid line. Of course, the most intriguing point was that of substitution—the solid-line for zero and the broken-line for one—where Eight Diagram system became the first perfect binary system of the world according to the natural process of development by Fu Hsi. The pattern of 0, 1, 2, 4, 8, 16, 32, 64, 128, and so on are in binary scale; they are equal to $2^0, 2^1, 2^2, 2^3, 2^4, 2^5, 2^6, 2^7$, and so forth. This true binary system is still used for the development of the computer in our time.

(Even today, most of Fu Hsi's works are still located at Huai Yang county of Hunan province of China.)

The significance of the Yin and Yang relationships is also clearly expressed in the special theory of Relativity of Albert Einstein (1879–1955). In addition to the above, the Yin and Yang system denies that the world is static and absolute. Time and space are not independent—they are mutually complementary. The Theory of Relativity acknowledges that frames of reference are relative, and that one is as good as another. All motions are relative. In the world of relativity we cannot speak of anything objectively without making reference to its relationship with the other. This idea is the central secret teaching of the Yin-Yang relationship within any system. Yin is always relative to Yang, and Yang is relative to Yin in all circumstances. Yin loses its meaning when its relationship with Yang is lost. Yang is Yang because of Yin.

Another one of the most interesting phenomena, which both the Tao of *I Ching* and modern science share, is that of what I term "Complementary Opposites." According to the Tao of *I Ching*, everything consists of all things. In other words, when there is Yin, there must be Yang. One does not exist without its counterpart, and the extremity of one converts itself into the other.

This idea seems to be realized in quantum mechanics as well. One of the most important discoveries that Paul Adrian Maurice Dirac of Cambridge made deals with anti-electrons. This discovery began with his study of space as the limitless sea of electrons, negative energy. However, later he found a "hole" which is known as the negation of an electron, a positive change. Subsequently, more than fifty particles were discovered and are known as "antis." As Heisenberg said, "Thanks to Dirac's discovery, i.e., [we have] the existence of antimatter." In the history of modern science, the discovery of counterparts was certainly an important event which strangely coincides with the view of Yin and Yang system. When there is positive, there is also negative. Matter seems to presuppose the existence of its counterpart, in this case, antimatter.

Hence arises the question, "What makes up matter?" For the Chinese the answer is simple: "Chi." Let's take a closer look at the well shielded and proven values of Chi. Using Chi to massage and to rejuvenate the energy is a well established and protected secret of Chinese Taoism. According to their definition, Chi is the combination of the four following components:

1. Sperm Chi;

2. Fetal Chi;

3. Atmospheric and Hydrospheric Chi (such as the air we breathe and the water we drink);

4. Earth Chi (such as the food we eat).

The first two types of Chi happen before childbirth during the binding of sperm to the egg, egg cell activation, changes in the pH of the cytoplasm, cell division, the development of the embryo, and so on. The last two kinds of Chi are created and developed after birth and are involved the respiratory, circulatory, and digestive systems.

Sperm Chi, also called the Fertilization Chi, is produced during fertilization—fertilized by sperm (Yang) in the oviduct, the ovum (Yin) becomes a fertilized egg. Even though several hundred sperm are needed to initiate many of the chemical changes required for fertilization, by penetrating the membrane, dropping the tail, preventing other sperm cells from entering, only one (1) sperm fertilizes the ovum. Smaller than a period, that tiny one (1) egg initiates cell division — from one into two (2) cells, to four (4) cells, to eight (8) cells, to sixteen (16) cells, and so on. That pattern of cell division (0, 1, 2, 4, 8, 16, 32, 64, 128, 256, 512, and so forth), which results in a rapid increase in the number of cells until they have specialized to form skin, bones, blood vessels, the brain, and so on, is one superb impetus for the research study on Chi and Tao of *I Ching*.

The Fetal Chi, also called Fetation Chi, comes about during the embryo development stage and plays an important role for the fetus until childbirth. It partakes in such actions as moving nutrients and waste products which pass between the placenta and embryo, driving the movements inside of the umbilical cord—which is connected to the network of embryonic blood vessels—to the circulatory system of the developing embryo, and so on. Deeply affecting, Chi moves around slowly inside the Fetus.

Atmospheric and Hydrospheric Chi are essential to all living beings. For example, the air we breathe in the internal and external respiration system and the water we drink for the circulatory system—which includes blood, blood vessels, the lymphatic mode, and so on—are all carried by either Atmospheric or Hydrospheric Chi.

After childbirth, all the food the child eats is vital for human body development. It is carried by Earth Chi throughout the body for cellular and/or internal respiration to create energy or to exchange carbon dioxide and oxygen between the circulatory system and the tissues of the body.

In general, Chi's functions can be subdivided into five inclusive types as follows:

1. Movement Type Chi

Chi is the source of all movement in, around, and out of the body. Breathing, the heartbeat, walking, dancing, eating, speaking, thinking, rejoicing, dreaming, growth, birth, maturation, aging, and so forth, all depend on the normal flow of the movement of Chi.

2. Transformation Type Chi

Chi is the source of harmonious transformation in our body. When food is ingested, it is transformed into other substances, such as blood, Chi itself, tears, sweat, and urine. These important changes depend on the smooth function of the transformation Chi.

3. Warming Type Chi

Chi warms our body. Maintenance of normal heat inside either our body as a whole, or any part of our body, such as the limbs, all depends on the function of warming Chi.

4. Protection Type Chi

Chi protects our body. By breathing normally, we can reduce excess anger, fear, or fright.

5. Governing Type Chi

Chi governs the body's substances and organs. Chi keeps everything inside our body in the proper place, such as the blood in the blood pathways. It also prevents excess loss of various bodily fluids, like sweat, saliva, and so forth.

Even though no American or English word or phrase can adequately capture Chi's meaning, when talking about Chi, it is very useful and important to remember that Chi is also directly related to the ever-moving and ever-changing universe whose movement is the result not of a creator, but of an inner dynamic of cyclical patterns—this is the nature of Tao.

The Original Meaning of Tao of *I Ching* is many-fold. The central idea that governs the Tao of *I Ching* is the concept I (易). According to Chinese etymology, the word "I" has three distinctive but interdependent definitions:

> 1. I Chien (易簡)—ease and simplicity;
>
> 2. Pien I (變易)—transformation and change;
>
> 3. Pu I (不易)—invariability/changelessness.

If one observes carefully, all of these three have the word "I" (易) in common. Because it is common to all three definitions, the three are mutually interdependent.

So, we can summarize the meaning of "I" as: simplicity, transformation, and changelessness. These are the basic characteristics of the changing process of the Tao of *I Ching*.

The Tao of I is simple and easy. As it was said, "The Chyan, Heaven, knows through the easy. The Kuen, Earth, does things through the simple. It is easy, because it is easy to know. It is simple, because it is simple to follow. By means of easy and the simple the laws of the whole world are known." If one observes the Eight Trigrams cautiously, one can see that all the changes are due to the slight change of the line in them: The change of a Yin line (- -) is the basis of all changes. From the diagram to the sub-atomic structure where the change results from emission and addition of quantum, to dividing and untying are the simplest ways to change things in the world. That is precisely why the changing process in the Tao of *I Ching* is simple and easy.

The second characteristic of the Tao of *I Ching* is the way of transformation and change. It means to procreate new formations. It is the process of renewal and reproduction—always with new creation (not just the rearrangement of existing elements). It is the power to transform and recreate all things in the universe. Things can grow and decay, produce and reproduce, because "I" (the changing process) has the quality of transformation. It is eternally in the changing process.

In seeming contrast, the third basic characteristic of the Tao of *I Ching* is Changelessness. The classical definition of Change is "Change that is also changeless." It is true that changelessness is the opposite of change. But, the Tao of *I Ching* is constant, permanent, ongoing, unceasing, and eternal. The unchangeable nature within the Tao of *I Ching* expresses itself in the constancy and invariable order of the changing process. Water never flows from lower to higher ground, the sun never rises from the west, and the moon never goes against the sun. The nature of the changing process is clearly expressed in the very word "I" (易), which deals with the interrelationship between the sun (日) and the moon (月).

Using another etymological approach, the word "I" can be analyzed as a combination of two totally different words:

1. "陽" which means the sun;

2. "陰" which means the moon in its old form.

The Eight Trigrams are also expressive of the Tao of *I Ching*. As invented by Fu Hsi, the Eight Trigrams were rooted in Oneness. In the transformation process, they propagated Yin and Yang. Then, Yin and Yang, the complete interplay of two polar strengths, generated four forces. Finally, these developed into the Eight Trigrams and so on.

Eight Trigram's Binary Reading

Translation from binary to decimal
using 0 for ▬▬ , 1 for ▬ ▬. For examples:

▬▬ =111=7; ▬▬↑ =110=6; ▬▬ =011=3; ▬▬ =001=1; ▬▬ =000

Note From the center: 1) Reading the Trigram from bottom up; 2) Writing binary from left to the right⟶ 110, reading the binary values (1, 2, 4, 8, 16...) is from right to the left.

184

Appendix I

Advanced Tai-Chi Chuan Class at San Francisco State University

FIGURE A.1: *Students of Tai-Chi Chuan at SFSU*

For the advanced Tai Chi Chuan class, students earn two units by spending two class sessions a week practicing outside and one session in the classroom to learn about Chinese and martial arts culture and philosophy. With Mrs. Kuo, come rain or shine, class is never cancelled. Students' dedication shows especially on those wet, windy winter days in San Francisco.

The highlight of the semester is the beloved Chinatown Walk, where students get to explore the seemingly hidden temples, herb shops and dim sum restaurants, a wonderful music store, the fortune cookie factory, and the famous Chinese Cultural Center of Chinatown, San Francisco.

FIGURE A.2: *The group never fails to visit the famous Ross Alley to try hot, fresh fortune cookies.*

FIGURE A.3: *Students also visit the Chinese music store to understand music by experimenting with traditional instruments.*

FIGURE A.4: *Madame Kuo shows advanced Tai-Chi Chuan students Chinese cabbage, which provides good nutrition in winter.*

FIGURE A.5: *Bitter melon cools down your system in summer.*

In addition to regular practice of Tai-Chi Chuan, Simu teaches that good nutrition is essential for robust health and correct circulation of the Chi. Chinese culture is rich in wisdom about how to eat in harmony with changes in the weather and the seasons. For example, around the Fall Equinox, it's a good practice to eat snow ears (mushrooms) cooked with raw sugar and lotus seed. To prevent wind attack, it is good to consume the seasonal young, tender ginger (with thin pink skin) in a stir-fry with pork, beef, or lamb, or mushroom and tofu for vegetarians.

Mrs. Kuo also recommends the Ching Po Leang Formula, which contains dried pearl barley, dried lily bulb, dried lotus seed, dried dioscorea, dried fox nut, dried longan, and dried polygontum. This formula is good for the blood, warms the body, and is especially good for women after their menstruation to help strengthen the system. Astragalus is also good for the chi, water excess or bloating, and the kidneys. Dioscorea is good for the lungs. Lycii berry, Wolfberry, and Tang Kuei are also good household remedies.

In this Chinatown, San Francisco, herb store and your local pharmacy you can buy Tiger Balm and white flower liquid. Both are good for headaches, allergies, asthma, or for preventing drowsiness on a long drive. Although the author is not a doctor and there are no guarantees for these remedies, Chinese people use these remedies for everyday life and for emergencies.

FIGURE A.6: *Simu Kuo and students visit herb store in Chinatown.*

FIGURE A.7: *The author on a research trip to Wu Tang Mountain, 2002*
FIGURE A.8: *Simu Kuo with Tai-Chi Chuan students at the Great Wall of China, 2001*

FIGURE A.9: *The author brings students to a martial arts academy in Taishan, China, to exchange experiences.*

FIGURE A.10: *Tai-Shan students perform martial arts for American students.*

Appendix II

Alcohol Treatment for Minor Injuries
Sifu Kuo Lien-Ying

(In Chinese)

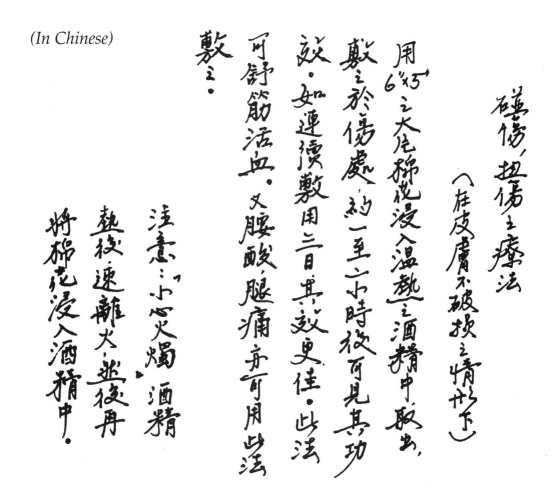

This treatment plan is very economical and effective if the directions are followed carefully. Also please keep in mind that this is a temporary treatment, and for more serious injuries, you may need to visit a doctor.

This treatment can be very dangerous because rubbing alcohol is extremely flammable and it creates a white flame that is invisible to the human eye. *Do not warm alcohol in a shallow pan over open flame or in the microwave; serious burns can result! The instructor accepts no responsibility for injuries that may result from improper preparation of medicines in the following handout.*

You need:

1. 70% or 80% isopropyl alcohol (rubbing alcohol)

2. A very tall, heat resistant pot with a lid

3. Cotton gauze (approx. 3″ wide and 12″ long, folded in half)

4. Plastic wrap

5. A towel or something to keep the area warm

Instructions:

1. Pour ⅓ of the bottle of alcohol into the pot, and place on *low* temperature on stove top: allow to simmer for 5–10 minutes (it is very important not to let the alcohol boil too vigorously for safety reasons). (*Note:* Heat is optional. Application of the alcohol wrap at room temperature is still effective.)

2. Allow to cool just enough as not to burn yourself when the alcohol is touched to the skin.

3. Place the gauze in the pot to absorb the alcohol.

4. Put the warm alcohol-saturated gauze on the area of the injury and wrap with plastic wrap (if you can, otherwise just keep the area warm).

5. Now is when you need a little patience: You must leave the gauze, plastic wrap, and whatever else is keeping the area warm in place for least 1 hour, and 2 hours would be better.

6. Repeat this procedure twice daily, until the pain subsides, for up to 3 days.

Hint: You must leave the gauze on the area for as long as possible—the longer the better.

Appendix III

Kuo Family Appreciation

Students bid farewell to the Kuos at Taipei airport.

Sifu and Simu Kuo with their son Chung-Mei in San Francisco.

Sifu Kuo Lien-Ying and Simu Simmone Kuo at Sifu's eightieth birthday party.

Poem honoring Simmone Kuo
—a gift from calligrapher Terry Luk

**Madame Kuo is dedicated to the martial arts
with great passion, artistry, and virtue.**

To Madame Simmone Kuo:

The Chinese Tai-Chi is
a gem and rare treasure
The 64 Fist is
so vigorous like a heavenly steed soaring across the skies
For many years you have selflessly passed on
this traditional art
Your patriotism and your devotion to martial arts
Your brilliance and hardworking have set a model
for us to follow

        —The Senior Tai-Chi Committee of the Yang Family School

                              Han Dan, July 2002

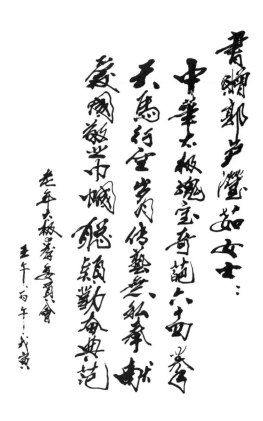

It is impossible for the tree to have a rest when the wind keeps
    blowing.
It is too late for the son to serve his parents when they are gone.

—Translated by professor JIN YU, *Yang Zhou University, China*

樹欲静而風不止
子欲養而親不在

In 1986, Simmone Kuo very proudly paid off debts incurred by her father
thirty-five years earlier. With this may his soul rest in peace.

神

非意所到可以識知日神

"A divine work is achieved not through human understanding, but by intuition."

不爭　不貪
不求
不自私　不自利
不妄語
萬佛城六大宗旨

No fighting, no greed,
no seeking, not being selfish,
no seeking personel advantage,
no lying.

— The Six Principles of the City of Ten Thousand Buddhas

Gift from Simu Kuo's mother, A-Hsiang W. Lu

Selected Bibliography

Beinfield, Harriet, L.Ac., and Korngold, Efrem, L.Ac., O.M.D. *Between Heaven and Earth: A Guide to Chinese Medicine*. New York: Ballantine Wellspring, 1991.

Blakey, R.B. & Yu-Tang, Lin. *The Saying of Lao Tzu*. China: Confucius Publishing Company.

China Reconstructs. Vol. XXXVIII No. 9, Sept. 1989. Beijing, China: China Int l. Book Trading Company.

Chinese Foods. Teacher's Handbook. San Francisco: Chinese Culture Foundation, Ethnic Heritage Studies Project, 1976, pg. 9–10.

Chun, Shin. *Chun-Tse Tai-Chi Chuan Tu Suo* Taipei City, Taiwan Province of China: Jun Sun Mei Publishing Co. 1967, pgs. 67, 69, and 73.

Editorial Committee of Shaolin Kung Fu. *Shaolin Kung Fu: Treasure of the Chinese Nation, the Best of Chinese Wu Shu*. China Pictorial Publishing House.

Hong Kong Hua Hsia Publications, ed. *Magnificent China*. Hong Kong: Hong Kong Hua Hsia Publications, 1972.

Jou, Tsung Hwa. *The Tao of Tai-Chi Chuan: Way of Rejuvenation, 5th ed.* Taiwan: Tai-Chi Foundation, Warwick, NY, 1991.

Legge, James. *Confucius: Confucian Analects, the Great Learning, and the Doctrine of the Mean*. New York: Dover, 1971, pg. 298.

Legge, James. *The Four Books*. New York: Paragon Press, 1966, pg. 948–950.

Low, C.C., ed. *Yue Fei. Pictorial Stories of the Great Chinese* National Hero, in Chinese and English. Singapore: Canfonian Pte. Ltd, 1991.

Pai-Shen, Ji and Lan-Tsung, Shi. *300 Tang Dynasty Poems: A New Translation English-Chinese*. Hong Kong: Chinese International and Hong Kong Business Press, 1987.

Palmer, Martin, ed. T'ung Shu: *The Ancient Chinese Almanac*. Boston: Shambalha, 1986.

Proverbs from the plaques on the bridge beside the Chinese Culture Center, Walter U. Lum Plaza in San Francisco Chinatown.

Ta Kung Pao. Hong Kong: Wen Tai Sun Chinese News Agency, 1990s Chinese medical information.

Walters, Derek. *The Chinese Astrology Workbook: How to Calculate and Interpret Chinese Horoscopes*. Northamptonshire, England: Aquarian Press, 1988. pg. 5.

Ware, James R., *The Sayings of Confucius*. China: Confucius Publishing Co.

Williams, C.A.S. *Outlines of Chinese Symbolism and Art Motives*. New York: Dover, 1976, pgs. 6, 85, 148, 150, 251, 275, 385, and 387.

Yee, Chang. *Chinese Calligraphy*. Cambridge, MA: Harvard University Press, 1973, pg. 196 and 222.